THE BAFFLED PARENT'S GUIDE TO
COACHING BOYS'
LACROSSE

Look for these other Baffled Parent's Guides by Ragged Mountain Press

Coaching Youth Baseball: The Baffled Parent's Guide,
by Bill Thurston

Great Baseball Drills: The Baffled Parent's Guide,
by Jim Garland

Coaching Youth Basketball: The Baffled Parent's Guide,
by David G. Faucher

Great Basketball Drills: The Baffled Parent's Guide,
by Jim Garland

Teaching Kids Golf: The Baffled Parent's Guide,
by Detty Moore

Coaching Youth Soccer: The Baffled Parent's Guide,
by Bobby Clark

Coaching Youth Softball: The Baffled Parent's Guide,
by Jacquie Joseph

THE BAFFLED PARENT'S
GUIDE TO
COACHING BOYS'
LACROSSE

Greg Murrell and Jim Garland

Ragged Mountain Press/McGraw-Hill

Camden, Maine • New York • Chicago • San Francisco
Lisbon • London • Madrid • Mexico City • Milan • New Delhi
San Juan • Seoul • Singapore • Sydney • Toronto

*To my wife Maureen—lacrosse brought us together, and we've spent
many hours watching each other play and watching games together. To my
parents—for the endless hours of getting me to practice and watching me play.
A special thanks to my dad, who gave up his baseball glove and bat and
picked up a stick to help me and my brother learn a new game. To my sons
Josh and David—may you find the same joy in sports and in life that I have.*
GREG MURRELL

*To the two people I have shared so many good experiences with—
my sons Casey and Matthew.*
JIM GARLAND

Ragged Mountain Press

A Division of The McGraw·Hill Companies

10 9 8 7 6 5 4 3 2

Copyright © 2002 Ragged Mountain Press

Library of Congress Cataloging-in-Publication Data
Murrell, Gregory.
    The baffled parent's guide to coaching boys' lacrosse / Gregory
Murrell, Jim Garland.
        p.   cm.—(The baffled parent's guides)
    Includes bibliographical references (p.   ) and index.
    ISBN 0-07-138512-6
        1. Lacrosse for children—Coaching. I. Garland, Jim, 1948– II. Title.
    III. Series.
    GV989.17 .M87 2002
    796.347—dc21   2001007479

Questions regarding the content of this book should be addressed to
Ragged Mountain Press
P.O. Box 220
Camden, ME 04843
www.raggedmountainpress.com

Questions regarding the ordering of this book should be addressed to
The McGraw-Hill Companies
Customer Service Department
P.O. Box 547
Blacklick, OH 43004
Retail customers: 1-800-262-4729
Bookstores: 1-800-722-4726

This book is printed on 70 lb. Citation by R. R. Donnelley & Sons, Crawfordsville, IN
Design by Carol Gillette
Production by Eugenie Delaney and Dan Kirchoff
Edited by Jon Eaton and Jane Curran
Illustrations by Greg Murrell and Shannon Swanson, unless otherwise noted
Photo page 4 by John Strohsacker, photos pages 29, 30, 37, 38, 39, 40, and 41 (top) by Greg
    Murrell; all other photos by Mike Edge

Contents

Introduction

Lacrosse is the oldest sport in America. Developed by Native Americans, it was often used to resolve conflicts and heal the sick. Games were played on "fields" that ranged from one to fifteen miles in length, and they often lasted for days. The basic rules of modern lacrosse were established in the late 19th century, as were the first college and high school teams.

Lacrosse continues to grow in popularity. There are currently over 200,000 male players at the college, high school, and youth levels, nearly half of whom are younger than 14. This increasing popularity has created a demand for more teams, more leagues, and more coaches. With this in mind, we developed *Coaching Boys' Lacrosse: The Baffled Parent's Guide* to help beginning and experienced coaches teach the game of lacrosse and have a successful season. The activities and suggestions are designed to help you teach 6- to 13-year-olds the exciting game of lacrosse. As you begin to think about the season, questions will arise regarding organizing a practice, understanding the rules, teaching the skills needed, and actually playing the game. This book will help you on your way to successfully and confidently addressing all these needs and will help you have fun doing so.

Your players will arrive on the first day of practice with all kinds of expectations. How you address them will be crucial to their success and yours as well. Some players may be new to the sport, and others may have a wealth of experience and knowledge of the game. The advice and drills in this book take into account the differences in abilities of the players and are appropriate to the development of your youth players. All activities encourage maximum participation and are designed to promote success.

How to Use This Book

Coaching Boys' Lacrosse is a collection of lacrosse knowledge, teaching drills and games, and coaching techniques. The purpose of the book is to provide the opportunity for coaches of all levels to have a positive experience teaching the fastest game on two feet. New coaches will find a recipe for success for breaking down the ten-on-ten game into teachable units and activities, and experienced coaches will be offered a new look at teaching the great game they know and love.

The first three chapters will help the novice coach get started. Chapter 1, Creating an Atmosphere of Good Habits, includes suggestions on how to establish yourself as the coach, methods for promoting good habits on the field, and questions and answers about common problems facing youth lacrosse coaches. Chapter 2, Before Hitting the Field: Lacrosse in a Nutshell, describes the basics of the game, such as how many players are on the field, the rules, and how to modify the game to meet the needs of younger players. Chapter 3, Setting Up the Season, gives you information on how to solicit volunteers, develop team policies, and address uniform and equipment issues. Chapter 4, The Fundamentals of Lacrosse, presents an overview of the essential skills of the game and how to get started teaching them. Chapter 5, The Practice, suggests ways to prepare for practices and gives sample practice schedules for beginning, intermediate, and advanced players. Chapter 6, The Game, discusses how to approach your first game against other teams, including coaching conduct, player management, and tips on game management. Chapter 7, Dealing with Parents, offers strategies for what can be the most difficult aspect of youth coaching. Chapter 8, Fundamental Drills, includes activities to teach the fundamental building-block skills of lacrosse. Chapter 9, Offensive Drills, and chapter 10, Defensive Drills, proceed from there to introduce the concepts of team offense and defense by looking first at individual techniques and then progressing to gamelike situations.

Developing a Coaching Style

The skills, drills, and games included in this book have worked for us over the years and are a collection of our experiences and innovations in the game. Our teaching philosophy is designed around several fundamental beliefs about coaching. Coaching styles are as varied as people—some are very quiet, and others are animated. There is no one right way to coach, but there are wrong approaches. Try to provide a positive experience for your players by designing practices that include lots of small-group activities that are gamelike, provide hundreds of touches with the ball, and, most of all, are fun. Drills that keep kids moving will motivate players and reduce behavior problems. This helps to build a positive atmosphere and build team spirit.

Broadly speaking, beginner drills and games are developmentally appropriate for ages 6 to 8; intermediate, for ages 9 and 10; and advanced, for ages 11 to 13. Cast nothing in concrete, however. Kids learn the game and develop their motor skills at different ages. Use the drills and games that best address the needs of your team and your individual players, regardless of age group.

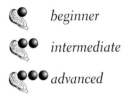

beginner

intermediate

advanced

Presenting information and activities to players and parents in a nondictatorial style and maintaining a positive temperament toward players, parents, and officials during practices and games will also help promote a positive experience for everyone. The ability of coaches to conduct themselves in this manner will be the measure of their success, not how many games the team has won. It also will send the important message that this is the behavior expected of everyone involved with the team.

Your number-one goal is fun—for you, your players, and the parents. How do you do this? There are five keys to being a good coach:

Come to practices prepared. Plan out your practices in advance so that you know what you want to accomplish during each practice. Determine what games and drills to use and how much time to spend on each one. Be familiar enough with each drill and game so that you can explain each activity to your players briefly but clearly. It's a good idea, especially with beginning and intermediate players, to walk them through the steps of a new drill so they'll understand what it entails. Most kids retain things better when they get a visual demonstration. If you take the time to plan out your practices in advance, your players will remain focused and interested throughout. And there's nothing wrong with writing down the plan for the practice on an index card to keep yourself organized during the practice.

Don't box yourself in: if your players aren't doing well with what you've planned, move on to something else. When the practice you planned isn't working, try a new activity or drill instead. Don't wait for players to get restless and lose interest.

Maintain a positive approach. Encourage your players by praising them when they've done a good job or made a good attempt. Reward them with a call of "Great work" or "Good try" or "Nice job." Be sure your players know that only you or your assistant should ever criticize a player. And if you feel you do need to correct a player, make your comments constructive, not negative. Positive encouragement will help all your players have a rewarding experience.

Show some enthusiasm. Start each practice energized, and encourage your players to keep up with you. By conducting your practices with a high level of energy, you'll transfer some of your excitement about the game to your players. Put some zip in your step and hustle onto the field to start your practice. Your energy will be contagious, and your players will put more into the practice because of it.

Get to know your players. Work on learning everyone's name as soon as possible. Players will respond positively when you call them by name. And pay attention to your players as individuals. Watch them as they interact with each other, and pay attention to their personalities. Keep the individuals in mind as you plan out your practices.

Who We Are

We've been active in youth sports for many years, and worked together to create the Motion Concepts Sports camps and clinics, where we teach the small-sided active learning philosophy illustrated in *Coaching Boys' Lacrosse*. Greg played lacrosse at Salisbury University. He is a coach with the boys' lacrosse team at North Harford High School and has been a staff member of the Harford County Lacrosse Camp for eleven years. He is currently the director of Motion Concepts Sports Camps, teaches middle school science in the Harford County Public Schools, and is completing a master's degree in administration at Loyola College.

Jim has been an elementary school physical education teacher for over thirty years. He holds bachelor's and master's degrees in physical education and a doctoral degree in child and youth studies. Jim is a member of Towson University's Athletic Hall of Fame, has coached youth and high school sports teams, and is the author of two other books in the Baffled Parent's series, *Great Baseball Drills* and *Great Basketball Drills*.

Coaching Boys' Lacrosse:
The Baffled Parent's Guide

CHAPTER 1

Creating an Atmosphere of Good Habits

The Essentials

One of the best ways you can provide a positive experience for your players is by creating an atmosphere of good habits. Your team will consist of many different personalities, and your players will have varying needs, abilities, and interests. In order for the players to have their best chances for improvement, and for you to have your best chances to teach, you and your players need some uniformity in procedures for practices and games. A disciplined learning environment provides everybody with the opportunity to get the most from the experience. Having a disciplined environment doesn't mean you have to be a dictator though. We've found the best way to create a positive atmosphere for learning is through something called the "My Job–Your Job" process. This is not an original idea, but one we've used over many seasons of coaching.

At your initial meeting with the players and parents (see Setting Up the Season, pages 18–19), ask them exactly what they expect from the experience. As they respond, write their suggestions on a chart everyone can see. Players probably will suggest things such as wanting to improve as players, getting adequate playing time in games, being treated fairly, etc. After everyone has had the opportunity for input, review each suggestion with the group. If there are any that you as coach cannot live with, discuss the issue until you can come to some kind of common ground. The final list of expectations that you, your players, and their parents agree to will be your guidelines for "My Job" as coach for the season. Make it clear to the group that you *will* meet these expectations. Giving players and parents an opportunity for input gives them ownership and helps foster a "we" atmosphere. It also makes expectations clear to everyone, so there's no confusion about the coach's role.

The second part of the process involves you stating your expectations of players and parents. These should also be written on a chart so that every-

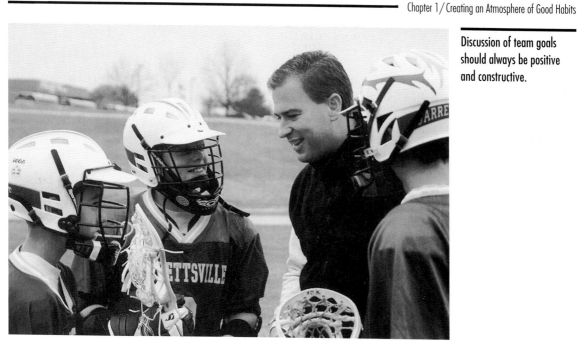

Discussion of team goals should always be positive and constructive.

one hears and sees your expectations. We've found that asking players and parents to respect the rights of others, to be honest with themselves and others, to do the little things right, to have the courage to make mistakes, and to be responsible are expectations that help produce an atmosphere of good habits. This is the "Your Job" part of the process for the players and parents. Discuss and refine these expectations until everyone is in agreement. Then ask the players and parents, "Will everyone who agrees to follow these rules please raise your hand?" This kind of public commitment to a common purpose helps serve as a contract between all parties involved.

The list you end up with should include individual player goals and team goals. During the season, have reviews after each practice and game where you and the players discuss these goals, praising good performances and suggesting possible solutions for problems that occurred. Don't emphasize winning and losing; instead, concentrate on the goals you and your team have established. Did the team achieve its goals? What about the goals of individual players? What worked? What didn't work? Why? Get your players to use their problem-solving skills to think creatively. From this review, you and your players will be able to come up with new goals for the next practice and the next game.

Remember that kids today want the same things they did thirty years ago when it comes to sports. They want to improve, they want lots of action, and they want to have fun. These things should help guide you in the daily planning of practices and games. By fostering team unity and spirit, helping your players work cooperatively, and appreciating them as individuals, you'll earn the respect of players and parents.

Winning and Losing

Some coaches feel that their role can be summed up in one word—winning. Regrettably, many parents, coaches, and players equate winning with success and losing with failure. It can be very difficult not to succumb to societal pressures about winning. Coaches who give in to the pressure to win will often be disrespectful to players, put all the best players on one team, give less experienced players less playing time than more experienced players, use ineligible players, and live and die with every call by the officials. Having a winning team and a losing team in each game is a reality. The issue then becomes how winning and losing are perceived and emphasized. Quite simply, being successful is winning, but winning may not lead to being successful. Being successful can be defined in many ways. Some would say that having the courage to participate and improving or showing progress are measures of success. We believe that you are successful if you accomplish the goals you establish with your team.

If you allow your team to think winning is their only goal, you'll set your team up for failure about 50 percent of the time. However, if you shift your emphasis from winning to accomplishing clearly defined goals during each practice and game, you'll teach your players to broaden their perspectives, learn about the game, improve their skills, and experience the fun and excitement of being a team. Remember that your players will take their cues from you, so give them good examples to follow. Emphasize that it's the overall experience that's important, not just winning individual games.

Promoting Teamwork, Concentration, and Good Habits

You can promote concentration and focus by limiting talking, keeping directions simple, and providing opportunities for lots of action in small-sided drills and activities that vary formations, number of players, skills, and tactics. Try to keep the various drills to limited segments of time (short, sweet, and to the point).

Hustle Contract

One of the best ways we have found to encourage players to establish good habits in practice and games is by having a *hustle contract*. This is a verbal agreement between coaches and players that simply says the coaches will hustle (enthusiastically prepare and implement practice and game plans) and the players will hustle (enthusiastically carry out the practice and game plans). You and your players take an oath by raising your right hand and saying, "I [name] will hustle in everything I do." During the season if you see players not responding quickly to directions, remind them gently: "Remember we have a hustle contract."

Huddling

Coaches need a way of keeping kids' attention. A method we've used successfully is called *huddling*. Huddling is a way of gathering the whole group together for instruction or other informational purposes, and it's also a good way to end practices. You and your assistant may use whistles to start and stop action during small-group work. We suggest you use two strong whistle blasts as the signal for all players to huddle as one group so that your players know the difference between stopping and starting and when you want to call the players to a huddle. Give the players 10 seconds to get to the huddle spot. If they all arrive in 10 seconds or less, the team scores 1 point. If they don't, you earn 1 point. At the end of the practice, if the players earn more points than you, they've earned a reward. Make the reward something simple like 5 minutes of extra shooting practice or 5 minutes of extra scrimmage time. Kids love to shoot and they love to scrimmage, so you'll be surprised at how well they respond to these little perks. We don't believe in physical punishment for the players, such as doing push-ups or running laps. Coaches have varying opinions concerning this issue, but we feel taking a positive approach helps promote a more positive atmosphere.

To help keep kids' attention, position the huddle away from distractions such as a bleacher full of spectators, another team practicing, or an entrance to a field where people are coming and going. Always stand so the sun is facing you, so the players can have good eye contact with you without looking into the sun. If there is a particularly anxious player on your team, position yourself near him when giving instructions. This will help prevent him from losing focus. If a player is doing a particularly good job listening, praise him. Say something like "Wow! I really like the way Joe is being a good listener today." This helps the entire team focus.

Good Listener Award

To help your players learn to value being good listeners, give out a good listener award. You might want to use your team name for the award. If your team name is the Tigers, make it the Tiger Award. This award is given to the player who demonstrates the best listening skills during each practice. You may want to expand the award to reflect the team expectations of respecting others, being responsible, and so on, with listening being one of the criteria in doing the little things right. Select a player at each practice to receive the award. This player then has the opportunity to select something from a list developed by you and your players as a reward for doing a great job. You might include such rewards as 5 minutes of extra instruction with the coach, extra shooting practice, or selecting the warm-up activity for the next practice. Players will want the recognition of earning this award, and their listening and concentration skills will improve. Be sure to emphasize that there can be only one winner at each practice and that not winning doesn't mean someone wasn't a good listener. Make sure to select players who really deserve the award; rewarding a player who hasn't met the criteria will have a negative effect on team spirit. And try to spread the award around so that everyone wins it at least once.

Questions and Answers

Q. What do I do about a player who is always late to practice?

A. At the initial meeting with parents and players, one of your expectations should have been the importance of starting practice on time. However, we don't think it's fair to penalize a player for something he can't control. Many players rely on parents to drive them to practice. Talk to the parents to see if there are circumstances preventing them from meeting their responsibility to have their child at practice on time. If other family commitments, work schedules, or other conflicts are making it difficult for them to be punctual, try to arrange another way for the player to get to practice, maybe with another teammate. Try to encourage carpooling—it can build friendships and camaraderie.

Q. Sometimes when my players are in the huddle and one of them is talking, other players begin talking. How do I handle this?

A. There is no room for disrespect among teammates and coaches. Talking when someone else is expressing an opinion or asking a question is a sign that what this player is saying is not valued by the teammate who is being disruptive. This should not be tolerated. Simply say "Excuse me" to the player asking the question and remind the disruptive player that one of the team rules is to respect the rights of others. Usually this is all that's necessary to regain focus. Then let the player who was asking the question continue. If the disruptive player continues to talk, let him know this isn't acceptable by calmly asking him to remove himself from the huddle. Before beginning the next activity, take the player aside, encourage him to follow the team rules, and ask him to rejoin the team. If the negative behavior continues, it will be necessary to have a meeting with the player and his parents to discuss a solution to the problem.

Q. Some of my more highly skilled players are beginning to criticize players on the team for being less skilled. What do I do about it?

A. One of your team expectations should be to respect the rights of others. All players have the right to try to improve their skills, no matter what their current level of skill is. At no time should a player criticize another player. This damages team spirit and the "we" atmosphere you are trying create; it should not be tolerated. Remind players who are critical of other players about the team rules and encourage them to be "helpful" and not "harmful." Nobody enjoys playing poorly. Encouraging a struggling teammate might be exactly what is needed to motivate that player to continue to try to improve. As each player improves individually, the team improves collectively.

CHAPTER 2

Before Hitting the Field: Lacrosse in a Nutshell

Lacrosse has been called the fastest game on two feet. The constant action and speed at which the game is played is appealing to players at all levels. This chapter gives an overview of the basics of the boys' game, including a description of the field, rules, and how to get started.

The Field

The lacrosse field is rectangular, similar to a soccer or football field (see next page). The official lacrosse field is 110 yards long and 53½ to 60 yards wide. (See our recommendation for the appropriate field size for young players on page 16.) A line in the center of the field (the *centerline*) extends from sideline to sideline. At the midpoint of this line is an X. This is the designated spot for face-offs. This centerline is marked 55 yards from each end line. A 6-by-6-foot goal is positioned on a line 40 yards from the midpoint of the centerline and 15 yards from the end line on each side of the field. Each goal has a 9-foot-radius circle around it known as the *crease*. Twenty yards from the centerline and parallel with it on each side of the field is a *restraining line*, which extends from sideline to sideline. The restraining line and the end line are the front and back boundaries of the *restraining box* or *goal area*, the sides of which are parallel with and 10 yards inside the sidelines. The restraining box or goal area thus defined at either end of a field of standard size is 35 yards deep and 40 yards wide. A line extended 10 yards to each side of the centerline, parallel with the sidelines and 20 yards from the center of the field, designates *wing areas*.

The Ball

The lacrosse ball is made of solid rubber. It is usually white, which makes it easier to find in tall grass. Sometimes orange or yellow balls may be used for more visibility, depending on weather or light conditions. A white ball must be used in games at the high school and college level, but leagues for younger players may not require a white ball.

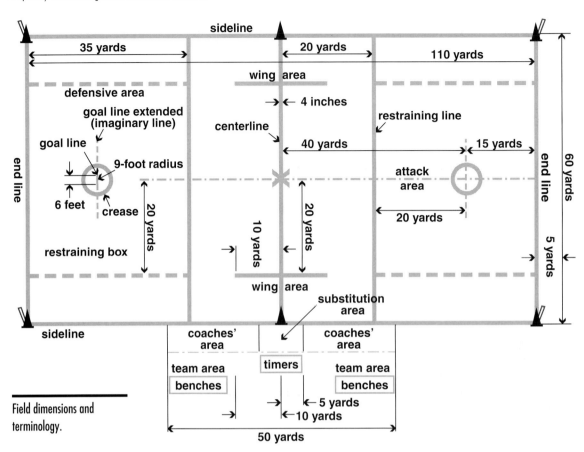

Field dimensions and terminology.

Equipment

Playing equipment for boys' lacrosse includes a helmet, mouth guard, elbow pads, rib pads, shoulder pads, gloves, and athletic supporter and cup. Additionally, goalies should wear a chest protector and throat protector; thigh pads and shin pads are optional. Special footwear is optional; many players wear molded cleated shoes similar to those worn in soccer and football.

Lacrosse sticks come in many different styles. They consist of molded plastic stick heads with composite or titanium shafts. Stick heads are generally strung with leather, although mesh pockets are sometimes more suitable for beginning players because the mesh forms a pocket easier. (See How to Determine Proper Fit for Equipment, pages 22–25.)

Players

A lacrosse team generally consists of 18 to 20 players. Ten players are on the field at one time; the rest are substitutes. The team on the field consists of one goalie, three defenders, three midfielders, and three attackers.

The *goalie* is the player most responsible for stopping opponents' shots. He is also the player who will begin the transition from defense to offense after he makes a save.

The *defenders* help in the goal area by defending opponents. When playing player-to-player defense, each defender is assigned an opposing attacker to defend.

The *midfielders* are responsible for defending their goal area, but they are also used on offense. These versatile players do the most running during the game because they are responsible for the full field, whereas the defenders and attackers basically are restricted to the defensive and offensive half of the field, respectively.

The *attackers* generally stay in their team's attacking half of the field. Their responsibilities are mostly offensive—to set up and score goals—although in transition they have defensive responsibilities as well.

Substitutes are used frequently, particularly at the midfield positions, where players do the most running. That's why teams generally need 18 to 20 players.

Scoring

One point is scored for each goal. A goal is scored when the ball passes over a line between the sides and under the top bar of the goal. The team with the most points at the end of the game is considered the winner. A sample scorebook page is shown on page 130.

Length of Game

Game length varies according to leagues. Some leagues play by quarters, some by halves. Many recreation programs have instituted running clocks as opposed to stop clocks because of time constraints. We recommend a running time of 8 minutes for beginning players (ages 6 to 8), 10 minutes for intermediate players (ages 9 and 10), and 12 minutes for advanced players (ages 11 to 13). The clock stops for time-outs, injuries, when the ball goes out-of-bounds, after a goal, and in the last minute of each quarter.

Basic Rules

Rules are sometimes modified for different leagues and different levels of play according to the needs of the players. Here are the basic rules to get you started. Check with your league officials regarding any modifications.

Body checking is allowed and is a way of stopping a player with or without the ball by making contact with an opponent's body. A player may check an opponent who is within 5 yards of a loose ball or a player in possession of the ball. The check must be from the front or side, and the contact must be below the shoulders and above the knees. The player's feet may not leave the ground during the body check, and he may not lead with his head.

Stick checking is another way to stop an opponent. A player may hit an opponent's stick with his own stick in an attempt to dislodge the ball. There are some restrictions. A player is allowed to strike only the stick and the glove of the opponent, not other parts of the body. Striking the opponent's glove repeatedly is a penalty. Striking the opponent's glove repeatedly or striking other parts of the body is called *slashing* and is not allowed. There are also restrictions on swinging the stick without control. Swinging the stick like an ax or baseball bat is considered out of control and results in a slashing penalty.

Certain actions aren't allowed in the game of lacrosse and result in either a personal or technical foul. *Personal fouls* are generally those actions committed by a player against an opponent, including slashing, tripping, body checking from the rear, or *cross checking* (using the stick to contact and check an opposing player's body). Unsportsmanlike behavior, although not necessarily directed at another player, is also considered a personal foul.

Technical fouls are penalties that include holding by a defender, interfering with the movement of a player who is more than 5 yards from the ball, pushing from behind, and being *offside* (not having three attackers in the offensive end of the field and four defenders in the defensive end of the field). It's also a violation for an opponent to be in the other team's *crease* (the circle around the goal) or to contact a goalie on his stick while he's in the crease.

How Penalties Are Assessed

For all personal fouls, the official will throw a flag. If the violating team is in possession of the ball, the official will blow the whistle and stop play. The violating player is removed from the game for 1 minute unless the aggressiveness of his act is excessive, in which case the official may remove the player for 2 or 3 minutes. In some cases, the severity of the penalty can result in expulsion from the game.

If the violating player is on the team without possession of the ball, the official will throw the flag but delay blowing the whistle to stop play. This "play on" situation continues until the team in possession scores, loses possession of the ball, or advances the ball inside the restraining box and then steps back outside the box with the ball. After one of these actions occurs, the official will blow the whistle, stop play, and give possession of the ball to the violating team's opponent.

The same procedure is used for assessing technical fouls. However, if the violating team's opponent has possession of the ball and scores, the penalty is waived. The penalty for technical fouls is 30 seconds. Common referee signals are shown on pages 128–29.

Getting Started

The game begins with a *face-off*, which takes place at the center of the field on a spot usually designated with an X. It's also the method used to restart the game after each goal is scored and at the beginning of each quarter. (See the section on face-offs on pages 39–40.)

To execute the face-off, two players from opposing teams, usually midfielders, face each other in a right-handed position (with their right hand at the top of the stick) with the head of their sticks facing in a back-to-back position and parallel to the midfield line. Their feet must be on the side of the midfield line that their team is defending and to the left of the head of their sticks. Both hands must be on the stick and must also be aligned to the left of the head of the stick. The sticks are positioned 1 inch apart so the ball may be placed between them. The official places the ball between the sticks, steps back, and blows the whistle. After the whistle is blown the two face-off players and the other midfield players then try to gain possession of the ball. When someone gains possession, the official signals the possession, and the attackers and defenders can leave their restraining boxes.

Play continues until a player scores or a team passes the ball over a sideline or end line. If this occurs, the other team is given possession of the ball. If a player in possession of the ball steps on or over an end line or sideline, the opposite team is awarded possession of the ball. If the ball is shot and goes out-of-bounds, the closest player to the ball when it crosses the line is awarded possession.

Players may substitute any time the ball crosses the sideline. If the ball crosses the end line or at any other time while the ball is in play, players can substitute *on the fly*. This means a player steps off the field into a designated substitution box, and his substitute enters the field from that box. Offensive players must enter and exit from the offensive side of the box. Defensive players must do the same from the defensive side of the box. Failure to do so by either offense or the defense results in an offside penalty. Midfielders can enter and exit from either side of the box. Players may also substitute when the whistle blows for a foul and at the end of each quarter and for time-outs. Each team receives two time-outs per half.

During play, each team must keep at least three players in its offensive half of the field and four players in the defensive half. Failure to follow this rule results in an offside penalty.

Game Modifications

Game modifications involve changing such things as rules, field size, equipment, length of game, and number of players. We recommend modifying the game to meet the players' needs at the beginner and intermediate levels. The advanced levels should play the official game on a regulation field, with the

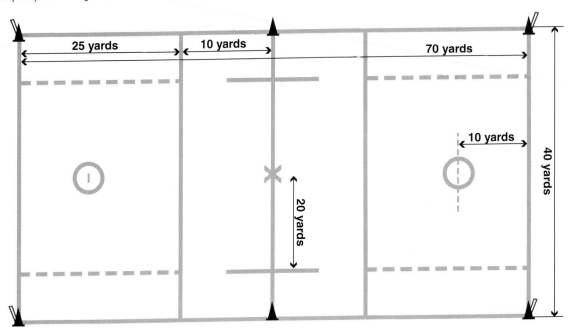

Modified field dimensions.

only exception being to reduce the time of play to 30-minute halves with a running clock.

    We recommend that the beginner-level game be modified by reducing the size of the field to 70 yards long and 40 yards wide (see illustration), playing with six field players and one goalie, eliminating the offside rule by allowing all players to move wherever they want on the field, and disallowing any checking, to reduce the possibility of injury. At this level players need to focus on developing skills and concepts instead of becoming confused by the names of positions, terminology, and the implementation of too many rules and structure.

    We recommend that the intermediate-level game be modified by disallowing checking and by reducing the time of play to four 10-minute halves.

    Of course, different leagues have the option of modifying the game according to the needs of the players in that league. The modifications we suggest are just recommendations. In making changes, the league should be guided by what will benefit the players.

Questions and Answers

Q. What should I do if a girl wants to play on our team?

A. Although similar in some aspects, boys' lacrosse differs significantly from girls' lacrosse. Both experiences will allow an individual to play with friends, develop concepts of space and movement, increase aerobic capacity, and improve skills. The girls' game differs significantly, however, in that there are no pads worn (except for the goalie) and no body checking is allowed. There are many other rule differences, such as out-of-bounds, restraining lines, and defensive rules. If there are no girls' lacrosse programs available in your community, then it's a question of whether the girls can participate at all in lacrosse; we believe they should have the opportunity to participate. If, however, girls' programs are available, then it's a question of which experience would better prepare the girls for involvement in later years, perhaps on the high school level. In this case, we believe that the techniques, tactics, and rules have such considerable variations from boys' lacrosse that most girls would benefit more from playing in the girls' program, unless they intend to play in a program in later years that uses the boys' rules.

CHAPTER 3

Setting Up the Season

Coaches of youth lacrosse teams have many responsibilities. These may include registering players; teaching skills, concepts, and strategies; ordering and maintaining equipment; purchasing and maintaining uniforms; manicuring fields; transporting players; contacting officials; scheduling practices and games; and developing cancellation procedures. Each of these is important and takes a lot of organizational skills, time, and effort. Of course, you might not be responsible for all of these tasks. If you're affiliated with a school program, an athletic director may assume some of the responsibilities. If your team is part of a recreation program, there's generally an official who plans the schedule.

As we suggested in chapter 1, the first step in preparing for the season is holding a meeting with the parents and players before the first practice. Make an effort to contact each parent personally before this meeting. This helps you get to know each parent and helps put parents at ease. One of the questions you should ask parents when you phone is whether their child has any health problems you should know about. It's important to know, for example, if a player is allergic to bee stings or if someone has asthma. If there are players with health concerns, get more details about how you can make their lacrosse experience a safe one. Ask these parents in particular to attend the first meeting. Let all the parents know that their input will be valuable in developing the team philosophy.

At the preseason meeting, provide a questionnaire for parents to fill out, supplying such information as their home address, home and work telephone numbers, and the name of a person you can contact in case of an emergency. Ask for their occupation, interests, or any specific skills they might have, including previous experience coaching or playing lacrosse, and whether they're willing to volunteer.

If practice and game schedules are arranged by league officials, an athletic director, or a recreation department representative, distribute copies of the schedule to parents and players at the meeting. This will help them plan for the season and possibly rearrange other family obligations that might interfere with attendance. If there's flexibility concerning times for practices or games, find out what times work best for the parents and players and see if those times will fit your own schedule. Try to plan practices twice a week and games once a week. Practicing more than twice a week may place a burden on families with other responsibilities. Practicing less than twice a week will make it difficult for players to improve their skills and learn team systems and strategies.

Also at this meeting, work with the parents and players to develop a list of expectations for each other. (See The Essentials on pages 6–7 for a discussion of establishing expectations.) After the meeting, write a letter to the parents in which you restate these expectations, reinforcing and reminding them of the "My Job–Your Job" process. Also include in the letter the names of team members and coaches, telephone numbers, emergency contact numbers, the schedule of practices and games (if you haven't already given this out), and a reminder about the commitment of parents and players to the team philosophy and goals. (See the sample letter on page 79.) Before distributing any personal information, such as telephone numbers, be sure to ask the parents' permission.

The preseason meeting is a perfect opportunity to outline for the parents all of the activities and duties you'll need their help with. Let them know how much their contributions to the team would be appreciated. Provide a sign-up sheet that lists the types of services they can help provide. You may want to have a parent as a general manager to coordinate all of the volunteer activities such as fund-raising, team dinners, uniform purchasing and distribution, snack bar commitments, field maintenance, and phoning players with team messages. That way you only have to communicate directly with one person if a question or problem should arise. (See the sidebar on page 80.)

It's extremely important that you don't alienate parents when soliciting them as volunteers. Don't dictate responsibilities—allow parents to have ownership in the decision making. Let them know that you're aware of how busy their lives already are. A pat on the back, a word of thanks, a "Great job!" before or after practice, or a note in the team newsletter will go a long way toward making them feel appreciated, and will encourage them to continue their support in the future. We all like to be praised for our efforts.

Occasionally you'll have parents who don't want to be involved. That's OK. That's something you can't control. Your job should be to let parents know in a courteous manner that help is needed and would be appreciated. Often parents don't volunteer because they aren't asked or because the team's needs aren't clearly defined.

You may also encounter parents who disagree with you. They may not like the way you organize practices or substitute players during games. This may occur in spite of their agreeing with the team philosophy at the preseason meeting. Discuss with these parents what you value in working with youth sports. See if you can come to some common ground about which approach best benefits the players on the team. In this process it's essential that you become a good listener. Let them have an opportunity to express their opinions. If your efforts fail in winning them over, let them know that it's OK to disagree. The manner in which they choose to disagree is the most important issue. Thank them for talking to you about whatever issue is concerning them. Let them know you appreciate their input but that you'll continue to function in the manner that was agreed upon by everyone at the preseason meeting. (See also chapter 7, Dealing with Parents.)

Selecting an Assistant Coach

Having one or more assistant coaches will be an integral part of your being able to implement a small-sided approach, including station work. Having an assistant will allow you to teach different skills at the same time or the same skills to players with varying levels of ability. The parent questionnaire distributed at the preseason meeting will be a good resource, offering information about any coaching and/or playing experience and their availability and desire to become involved. However, these are not the only criteria for selecting an assistant coach. Most important is how any potential

Tryouts

Kids love to play. Although they exhibit many similarities, there are certain to be differences in ability because their rates of development vary. The best example we can think of is Michael Jordan being cut from his high school basketball team. Of course, you know how that story turned out!

We don't think that tryouts should be used on the youth recreational level. Every child interested in playing should be given the opportunity to play, regardless of ability. We encourage coaches to do their best to make each player's experience with lacrosse a positive one. Save tryouts for other more competitive experiences such as travel leagues, club teams, and high school sports. If you're coaching one of these more competitive teams, ensure that tryouts are organized so that all players

- have a clear understanding of the expectations

- have the same opportunities for success

- are assessed according to objective standards (they can throw and catch efficiently) as opposed to subjective standards (their hair style is different from the other players')

- are treated with dignity

Be sure that players understand that you're critiquing their playing ability and not them personally.

We've found the best way to handle players who don't make the team is to treat them the same way as players who do. That is, meet with them individually, clearly explain their strengths and weaknesses, and suggest a plan for improvement.

Skill Assessments and Positions

Players who are 6 to 13 years old are eager to play lacrosse and like to try playing different positions. Don't squelch this enthusiasm by deciding a player is not sufficiently skilled to play a particular position, unless safety is an issue (for example, a player wants to play the goalie position, but his reflexes haven't developed to where he can move the stick fast enough to avoid getting hit with the ball). Players at this age develop at different rates. No one can tell with certainty what kind of skill level and athleticism a 6-year-old player may exhibit in the years to come, especially if this player is immersed in a positive environment where he's engaged in a variety of experiences. Generally, coaches who allow players to play only certain positions at very young ages have their own interests as a priority (e.g., winning), instead of the interests and development of their players. What these coaches fail to realize is that winning is only a short-term goal. Most young players will be involved with lacrosse for five to ten years, or maybe even longer. So "winning" would be better defined as helping players prepare for the long term. Coaches should ask themselves this question: What do I want my lacrosse players to be able to do by the end of their careers? By starting with the endpoint in mind, it's easier to plan how to get there and guarantee success.

assistants treat other people. Do they have a positive, friendly manner? Are they courteous with the players? Look for someone who interacts positively with you, your players, and parents, and treats everyone with mutual respect. If necessary, you can help them train for coaching, or you can suggest other ways for them to prepare, such as reading books, watching high school, college, and professional games, and attending lacrosse coaching clinics.

Equipment

As discussed in chapter 2, there's a lot of equipment needed in the game of lacrosse. This is an area that needs to be addressed early if equipment needs to be repaired or purchased. Depending on availability, some equipment may take eight to ten weeks or longer to be delivered. One of the first things you should do is inventory the team equipment. Make a list of equipment in need of repair or replacement and estimate what the costs will be. It may be necessary to solicit donations from parents or sponsors or to plan a fundraiser, which will take time to plan and implement. You also might want to check a local high school to see if they have any extra equipment to donate to your team. Because of the size of high school players, this usually works only with players who are 11 to 13 years old. However you decide to get your equipment, getting an early start will help ensure your team will be ready for the season.

To minimize expenses for parents, try starting a league inventory. Since youth players keep growing and will generally need new equipment each year, have players consider donating their used equipment to the league. This will help keep expenses down.

Other issues involving equipment include its distribution to players, collection after the season, and storage. A parent who has volunteered as the team's equipment manager can assume these responsibilities.

Remember to make sure your players stay well hydrated during practices and games. We suggest that your players be responsible for bringing their own water bottles. Discourage players from sharing water bottles with other players to reduce the spread of germs. You may want to have a parent volunteer in charge of providing a container of extra water so that players have plenty of fluids. Plan water breaks during practice, and make sure that players are drinking water during games.

How to Determine Proper Fit for Equipment

Most lacrosse equipment is made in a range of sizes for youth and adult players. In addition, there are different designs available so players can get the best fit.

Determining what works for your players is best accomplished by their trying on the equipment and evaluating the fit. Is it comfortable to wear? Does it cover the area of their body it is designed to protect? When worn with all the other gear, does the player have freedom of movement to pass, catch, scoop, and shoot? Ultimately it is a matter of choice. However, players should never compromise safety for style. The beginning player should choose the safest model, one that provides the greatest protection. Intermediate and advanced players may choose a style that provides more flexibility and that suits their position. Certain styles are designed with the position in mind, with safety still the number-one concern.

Gloves. Gloves come in a variety of sizes and styles. They are made of various materials, some for comfort and others for design. The key to selecting the proper glove is fit, which means the player's fingers should come close to the end of the holes. A glove that is too big makes it difficult to handle the stick properly. The fingers will slide in the holes, causing the player to lose his grip. Does the fit allow a comfortable grip on the stick? This may vary from style to style, based on the material used in making the palm of the glove. Other features to consider are the amount of forearm and wrist protection the glove provides and the amount of mobility it allows.

Arm pads. These are often difficult to fit. The elbows are very vulnerable to defensive checks and therefore require quality protection. Great improvements have been made in materials and fit over the past several years—the days of overstretched, taped-on pads are gone. Now players can choose from a variety of sizes and styles designed to protect and meet their flexibility and comfort needs. Players can choose pads that start at the glove and end at the shoulder pad or any degree of length in between. Arm pads should fit snugly and should allow for a full range of motion. Players should try the pads while wearing gloves and holding a stick. Make sure they can complete the motions of passing and scooping. The pads should not get caught on any other equipment.

Shoulder pads. There are a variety of sizes and styles for shoulder pads. Shoulder pads may have an added upper-arm extension that overlaps the arm pad or begins where the arm pad ends. This provides increased arm protection but may limit flexibility. Other pads have increased chest or shoulder padding. These increase safety to those areas and are designed with defenders in mind, although they're appropriate for all positions. Again, players need to try on equipment and check the fit and ease of movement.

Helmets. When fitting helmets, safety should be the main concern. The helmet should allow good vision in all directions and should fit snugly, without wobbling. If there's any movement, a smaller size is needed. Helmets come in several styles and sizes, measuring from extra small to extra large. If the helmet is uncomfortable, you can try using the inserts that sometimes are provided with the helmet.

All helmets should have a NOCSAE (National Operating Committee on Standards for Athletic Equipment) stamp of approval, which means they have been tested for safety. There are many stores that supply helmets, and they all have staff that can help players and parents decide which style is best. Emphasize to parents that safety is the main issue and that a higher price doesn't necessarily mean a higher level of safety. All new helmets meet rigid standards. Concerns could arise with older helmets, especially ones that are passed down from older players. Make sure you see the NOCSAE stamp of approval on all the helmets before players take the field.

Mouth guards. All players should wear a mouth guard (some leagues require them) to protect their teeth and lips and to soften blows that might cause concussions or jaw fractures. They attach to the face mask of the helmet. Preformed mouth guards can have an acrylic liner that molds to the teeth with use, or they can be softened by heating and then fitted by biting down on them. They also can be custom-made by the child's dentist.

Shoes. There are no requirements for special lacrosse shoes, although many players choose to wear a molded cleat shoe similar to those worn in baseball or football (however, metal cleats are not allowed). These tend to be the shoe of choice because they are typically a three-quarter height shoe or a high-top shoe. This style gives extra ankle support that may help a player change directions quickly. Many major shoe manufactures offer multiple choices in appropriate footwear for lacrosse. Choose a shoe that fits well and that's comfortable. When possible, players should choose a lightweight shoe.

Sticks. The parts of a lacrosse stick include the head, the sidewall, the pocket, the top string, the throwing strings, the sidewall strings, the neck, and the shaft.

The *head* of the stick is a plastic frame that connects to the handle or shaft by being screwed on at the neck. The actual shape of the head can aid players in several ways. Certain heads are designed to allow a deeper pocket

Head with open sidewall design.

top stringing

mesh lining

ball stopper

neck

sidewall stringing

sidewall

throwing or shooting strings

and therefore greater ball control, allowing the player better ball possession. Others are curved to allow for easier scooping ability. Some are designed to increase passing accuracy and facilitate quick release of the ball.

Plastic heads were introduced over three decades ago, and since then, the variety in head designs has exploded. When Greg began playing, he remembers only a few head-shape choices, and all heads were designed with closed sidewalls. Now there are many more choices. Sticks can have *open* or *closed sidewalls* (see illustrations). The closed sidewall design means a less flexible head, which many defenders prefer since the head maintains its shape better during checking. Some players also prefer a less flexible head for face-offs because it maintains its shape during *clamping* (see page 40). Open sidewall sticks, the most popular design, are lighter and more aerodynamic than closed-sidewall sticks. You'll notice that most sticks have at least a partially open sidewall.

Mesh pockets are similar to a net, and are preshaped and attached to the head by the sidewall stringing, the top string, and bottom string. The pocket is formed by breaking in, or softening, the mesh by repeated throwing and catching. Additional adjustments can be made by loosening or tightening the sidewall strings or the bottom strings. Tightening or loosening the strings changes the location of the ball in the pocket, causing the ball to release higher or lower, and affecting the power of the throw or shot. Loosening (lengthening) the throwing strings helps the ball stay in the pocket dur-

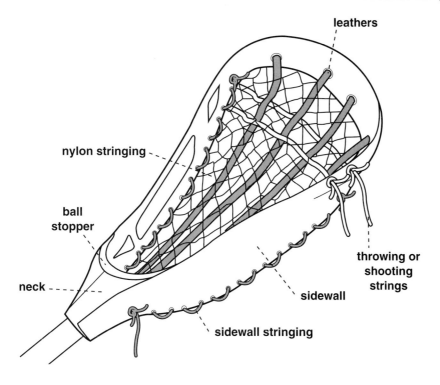

leathers

nylon stringing

ball
stopper

neck

throwing or
shooting
strings

sidewall

sidewall stringing

ing cradling or a stick ckeck. Each player usually has a slightly different pocket based on his own throwing or shooting. It may take players some time to learn just what shape of pocket is best for them. The traditional *leather pocket* is a combination of four leather strings attached at the top and bottom of the head. The leather runs parallel with the sidewalls. Nylon stringing is then woven in between the leathers.

Sticks for the beginning players are purchased prestrung. As players learn more about their own throwing and passing motions, they usually begin to experiment with stringing their own sticks. Kits are available with instructions and stringing materials. Usually one or two players on a team become "gurus" at stringing, and will string sticks for their teammates. As players become more familiar with their passing and shooting, they will also experiment with tightening or loosening their throwing or shooting strings, or adding additional throwing or shooting strings. Sticks become very personal items, and players will develop their own likes and dislikes as to stick makers and stick design. It's best to have players research and try out different designs. Manufacturers' Web sites are often a good resource.

Shafts are most often made from aluminum, titanium, or a composite. Attackers and midfielders use sticks that are 40 to 42 inches long. Defenders and long-stick midfielders may use sticks 52 to 72 inches long.

Questions and Answers

Q. If I can't find volunteers from my parent network, where can I go?

A. Volunteers don't have to come from your parent pool. We suggest you talk to your high school athletic director or lacrosse coach. Many high school players are willing to help younger players develop their skills. Other members of the community without children may also be interested in helping. Take out an ad in the local newspaper or place a poster asking for volunteers at the local supermarkets and convenience stores. Look for someone who will be a good role model and who will have a positive impact on your team.

Q. Where can I purchase lacrosse equipment?

A. Most local sporting goods stores have equipment available. If you're responsible for purchasing the equipment, you may want to consult with other coaches in the league to find out where you might get the best price and service. You might want to team up with several coaches when you place your order so that you get a volume discount. High school coaches are another source of information concerning where to purchase equipment and which brands have proven to be the most durable. (See the Resources section for more information.)

Q. Our facilities are limited. Our team was given only one night to practice during the week. Is this enough?

A. In most cases, no. Players need to acquire skills and concepts through repetition. Additionally, for many players practicing only once a week will affect their recall, and you'll find yourself repeating much of the information you covered the previous week. You might want to investigate other possible practice sites. You don't need a regulation field or even goals to accomplish lots of skill work with your players. Another alternative might be to approach a coach of another team in the same age group that practices on a different night. You can share the field both nights, resulting in two practices a week. You'll still run your own practices, plus you'll have the opportunity to end your practice with a scrimmage against the other team.

CHAPTER 4

The Fundamentals of Lacrosse

This chapter is divided into three sections. The first addresses fundamental skills that all players need to know. Included are the basic stick skills required for building individual confidence and team success. The second and third sections focus on the fundamentals of offense and defense, from basic formations to special situations. This chapter will introduce you to the basic skills your players need at the start of the season and for developing as a team. This information, combined with the fundamental drills, offensive drills, and defensive drills (covered in chapters 8, 9, and 10) will help you get started.

Essential Skills and How to Teach Them

Cradling

Cradling is one of the most difficult essential skills to master and involves keeping the ball in the pocket while running up the field or maneuvering through the defense. It's also one of the most important for all lacrosse players since doing it well means players have more opportunities to maintain possession of the ball. The motion of cradling involves the arms and wrists and has several basic principles (see photos, page 29).

The grip. Each hand is placed on the stick in a different way. The bottom hand is considered the control hand and is wrapped loosely around the bottom of the stick. The thumb of the bottom hand is also wrapped around the stick, which is important to note because the thumb's position on the top hand will differ. The top hand provides part of the motion that helps keep the ball in the pocket of the stick. The stick should rest lightly in the fingers to allow the stick to be curled slightly toward the wrist.

Wrist action. Beginning players often have difficulty with this. The motion of the wrist should be controlled and smooth. As players begin to cradle, the ball should stay relatively still in the pocket. If the ball is jumping or bouncing in the pocket, the wrist is moving too quickly, and the range of motion is too great. Have the player slow the motion and limit how far the wrist moves. The wrist can move about 150 degrees when curled out away from the body. Of this motion, 70 degrees is wrist extension, and 80 is wrist flexion, or being curled in toward the body. Beginning players should focus on moving the wrist no more than half that range. As they become more advanced, they'll learn when it's necessary to use a full range of wrist motion.

Arm action. The forearm of the top hand on the stick should swing like the movement of a hinged gate or door. Initially the swing may be long, but as players become more comfortable, the swing should decrease. The upper arm (from the elbow to the shoulder) should remain mostly stationary but may move as part of the natural running motion. The bottom arm and hand should move in concert with the top arm and hand as if attached by a string.

This action is used as the cradle changes to the vertical position from a more horizontal position.

Stick position. Players need to use several different stick positions based on the situation on the field. If a player is moving up the field without any defensive pressure, the stick may be in a more horizontal position. As defensive pressure increases, the stick moves to a more vertical position and should be parallel with the body.

One-arm versus two-arm cradling. Two-arm cradling is usually taught first because having two hands on the stick is more secure. It's used to keep the arm and wrist action under control. The two-arm cradle also allows the player to move more easily to the passing or shooting position. One-arm cradling is used once the player becomes more comfortable and has control of the cradling motion. The one-arm cradle becomes essential as defensive pressure increases. It permits increased mobility and allows the player to hide the stick much better from the defender.

Scooping

Scooping is getting possession of ground balls or loose balls (much like getting rebounds in basketball), and is a very important skill for your team to master. Most coaches analyze scooping statistics first when reviewing a game. Your players should use proper technique in scooping the loose ball and should be able to scoop with both hands, so you'll want to create an environment that challenges your players to excel at this skill. To encourage getting possession of ground balls, many teams reward the player who earns the most ground balls during a game or practice session. The ability to "win" the ground ball begins with hustle and ends with technique, and the fastest player does not always win the battle. (See Scooping Drills, pages 91–94.)

In order to win a ground ball, players have to anticipate the loose ball occurring and position themselves to pick up the ball once it's free. There are two situations that require slightly different techniques for scooping the

Top left: The beginning cradling position. The top hand is slightly down the shaft from the head of the stick. The wrist is straight. The bottom hand is near the end of the shaft.

Top right: The finishing cradling position. The top hand remains slightly down the shaft. The wrist has curled in toward the body, rotating the head of the stick. The bottom hand and arm have remained in relatively the same position.

Below left: One-handed cradling. The hand is positioned where the head meets the shaft. The stick is parallel to the player's body.

Below right: By rotating his body, the player shields his stick from the defender.

ball: uncontested ground balls and contested ground balls, where players "battle" for possession.

The Uncontested Ground Ball

Body motion. The player begins by running to the ball as quickly as possible. This allows him maximum time to win the ball. Once the player reaches the ball, several motions work in concert to complete the scoop.

The player bends at the knees and moves his midsection lower to the ground.

The player then extends the stick head toward the ball, aiming just behind the ball.

Stick position. The player's bottom hand also lowers, making the stick parallel to the ground. Many players have difficulty with this movement because they keep their bottom elbow too high, and so the stick is more perpendicular to the ground than parallel.

Finishing the scoop. The finishing motion is the scoop or shovel movement that moves the head of the stick through the ball and brings the head of the stick up toward the player's eyes. This should be a fluid (not a stabbing) motion where the player begins with the head of his stick just behind the ball and continues until the ball has settled into the pocket. By finishing

Top left: The player begins his approach by looking to see where potential defenders may be, then he locks in on the ball and attacks it.

Top right: Note the wide stance the player takes. He uses his legs to shield the ball, his back hand is down, and the head of the stick is just behind the ball.

Below left: When scooping the ball, the player explodes through the ball.

Below right: The player brings the ball to the box area and continues to move to open space, or he completes a change of direction away from pressure.

in this way, the player makes sure he's concentrating on the ball, and the ball ends up in the stick. Also, the motion of bringing the head of the stick toward the player's head allows for the best stick and ball protection and places the stick into the *box area* for passing. The box area is the space to the side of the player's helmet and above the shoulder. This area provides protection of the stick head and places the stick in the proper location to pass or to shoot.

The Contested Ground Ball

Body motion. The player begins by running to the ball as quickly as possible. This allows him maximum time to win the ball. Once the player reaches the ball, several motions work in concert to complete the scoop.

The player positions his body between the ball and the opposing player, creating a shield with his back and legs. This gives the player the best position to win the ball and also creates a possible penalty situation, because pushing from behind is illegal in lacrosse.

The player then bends at the knees and takes a slightly wider stance than if uncontested. This allows the player to use his legs to protect the ends of the stick from being checked while trying to scoop.

Stick position. The player finishes the play by extending the stick head toward the ball, aiming just behind the ball.

The player's bottom hand also lowers, making the stick parallel to the ground. Many players have difficulty with this movement because they keep their bottom elbow too high, and so the stick is more perpendicular to the ground than parallel.

Finishing the scoop. The finishing motion is the scoop or shovel movement that moves the head of the stick through the ball and brings the head of the stick up toward the player's eyes. By finishing in this way, the player makes sure he's concentrating on the ball, and the ball ends up in the stick. Also, the motion of bringing the head of the stick toward the player's head allows for the best stick and ball protection and places the stick into the box area for passing.

Passing and Catching

As is true in any field sport, the ability to pass and receive the ball individually and collectively as a team is essential for success. Players will develop the ability to use several different methods of passing and catching once they've mastered the fundamental techniques. Encourage your team to practice, practice, and practice these basic skills. It's amazing how much confidence players will have once they're sure the ball is going where they intended to throw it and once they can catch the ball routinely without dropping it. There are basic elements of passing and catching that should be emphasized at each practice. (See Passing and Catching Drills, pages 86–90.)

Passing

The stance. To begin, the player stands facing the player to whom he intends to throw the ball. His feet are offset. If the player is left-handed, his right foot is in front of the left. If the player is right-handed, his left foot is in front of the right. This positioning is similar to throwing a ball.

Trunk rotation. The player rotates at the waist so that his shoulders become perpendicular to the player to whom he intends to throw.

Hand position. The player's top hand is positioned near the head of his stick. The thumb of his top hand is extended up the shaft of the stick to help with accuracy. His bottom hand is located at the bottom of the stick and serves as a pivot point for the throw.

The throwing motion. The player pulls the stick back so that his top hand is positioned above the shoulder by about 6 inches. (Be sure that a young player doesn't bring the head of the stick back too far, like a catapult. This can result in the ball dropping out of the stick behind the player.) The player's top hand and arm push the stick forward in the direction of his teammate. His bottom hand provides the power for the pass. The player's hand and arm are about 6 inches from the body and across the waist. The bottom hand acts as a hinge or pivot and moves back toward the body slightly as the top hand and arm extend forward. The speed of the action determines the speed of the pass.

Finishing the pass. The player's top arm extends fully in the direction of the pass, which helps with accuracy. The player's front foot steps forward toward the teammate the player is passing to. His weight shifts from the back foot to the front foot as part of the step, which helps add power to the pass. The wrist of the player's top hand moves from a normal resting position to an extended position at the end of the throw. This can be demonstrated by having a player throw a pass with one arm and hand.

Catching

The stance. The player stands facing the player who is passing the ball. His feet are offset. If the player is catching left-handed, his right foot is slightly forward. If the player is catching right-handed, his left foot is slightly forward. The stance changes slightly once the ball arrives.

Stick position. As the player prepares to receive the ball, he holds his stick parallel to his body. His top hand is near the top of the shaft of the stick and is held slightly in front of his head. His bottom hand is in a similar position to passing. The player's arm is extended across the body at waist height, with the bottom hand slightly behind the top hand. The head of the stick should also be in the box area a few inches to the side of the receiving player's head.

Here it comes. The player's focus is on the ball as it moves toward him. Hand-eye coordination obviously is part of the process. The player watches the ball move into the pocket and tries to catch the ball in the box area.

The box area, which the coach is pointing to, is the area players pass from and try to pass to. This player's stick head has extra protection to shield it from a defender.

The stance changes. As the ball lands in the head of the stick, the player cushions the pass by easing the stick back from slightly in front of his head to even with his ear. His shoulders rotate slightly toward the side the ball is on. This motion helps the ball settle into the stick, and it also places the player in position to cradle, pass, or shoot.

Dodging

Regardless of a player's position on the team, it's important that all players understand the basic dodges of lacrosse. Whether they're trying to create their own space and attack the goal, or whether they're trying to clear past a riding attacker, these are skills that all players need to have, and there are different dodges to aid their success. (See Dodging Drills, pages 94–98.)

Roll Dodge

Beginning the dodge. The purpose of the roll dodge is to gain attacking space directly behind the defender. The attacking player moves with speed toward the defending player. The dodging player begins with two hands on the stick in order to remain a threat to pass or shoot. As the player meets the defender, the player drops the bottom hand off the stick and completes the dodge one-handed.

Stick position. The dodging player holds the stick parallel to his body and draws the stick into the body, with the head of the stick next to his head. The lower part of the head of the stick should be in the shoulder area. The player's shoulder and upper arm create a protective pocket for the stick. The elbow should be up and perpendicular to the body to help keep the stick parallel. The stick should not be presed against the body; this is a violation and results in a loss of possession.

Body motion. The left-handed attacker begins the dodge by stepping with the right foot. In the step phase, the foot is placed just in front and on an imaginary line located between the legs of the defender. The right-handed attacker begins by stepping with the left foot. The front foot is the plant foot and is the foot the player uses to pivot and complete the dodge. The back foot is the swing foot. The dodging player rotates his back foot away from the defender using his front foot as a pivot, and swings his back foot and his body so that his back is to the defender. The swing foot takes a position to the side of the player and beyond the defensive player's foot.

Finishing the dodge. The dodging player keeps the stick in front of his body. His next step is across the path of the defender, which places the defender directly behind the dodging player and allows the dodging player better stick protection and the most direct line to the goal. The player then explodes (accelerates) as he is exiting the dodge, keeping his eyes on the target. The dodging player should maintain stick protection until he gains space.

Top left: The player attacks at an angle, driving the defensive player.

Top right: Once the offensive player feels pressure, he steps into the defensive player with the foot opposite to the side on which he is carrying the stick. The player uses his shoulders and head to protect the stick and begins to roll away from pressure.

Below left: The offensive player pivots on the plant foot and spins his body away from pressure, stepping beyond the defender with the foot that is on the same side as the stick. This places the defender behind the offensive player, and space is gained.

Below right: The dodge is completed with the stick protected and the player exploding to open space.

Face Dodge

Beginning the dodge. The dodging player attacks the defender. As the space closes, the dodging player sets up the dodge by faking a pass or shot, which causes most defenders to raise their stick and come out of their defensive stance to a more upright position.

Stick position. The dodging player attacks and completes the dodge with two hands on the stick. The stick remains parallel to his body, and the head of the stick moves across his body from one box area to the opposite box area.

Body motion. The right-handed dodging player begins by planting his left foot just outside the stance of the defender. The next step occurs with the player's right foot stepping across the stance of the defender. The right foot is placed next to the defender's right foot and is used as the plant foot to explode past the defender. As the right foot begins its motion, the stick mirrors the foot motion as it moves across the body. The next step with the left foot is beyond the defender, placing the dodging player's body between the defender and the target of attack. The movements of the left-handed player would mirror these movements.

Finishing the dodge. The stick remains in the box area of the opposite side until open space is gained. The player can then use either hand to pass or shoot.

Split Dodge

Beginning the dodge. The dodging player attacks the defender. As the space closes, the dodging player sets up the dodge by faking a pass or shot, which causes most defenders to raise their stick and come out of their defensive stance to a more upright position.

Stick position. The dodging player attacks with two hands on the stick

Left: The player sets up the face dodge by having the stick in the box area, forcing the defender to anticipate a pass or shot. The defender raises his stick, and the dodge can be executed.

Center: As the player approaches, he draws the stick across his face from one box area to the opposite box area. This allows for quick movement and good stick position.

Right: The dodge is completed by the player exploding past the defender and keeping the stick in front of his eyes. Once space is gained, the player returns the stick to the box area for the pass or shot.

and completes the dodge with the opposite hand on the stick (a right-handed player ends with the stick in his left hand). The stick remains parallel to his body, and the head of the stick moves across his body from one box area to the opposite box area.

Body motion. The right-handed dodging player begins by planting his left foot just outside the stance of the defender. The next step occurs with the player's right foot stepping laterally outside the stance of the defender on the other side. The right foot is placed even with or beyond the position of the defender's left foot and is used as the plant foot to explode past the defender. The next step with the left foot is across the defender's body, placing the dodging player's body between the defender and the ball. The movements of the left-handed player would mirror these movements. The split dodge is similar to a face dodge, but it moves the defender a greater distance laterally and relies on the dodging player's quickness, not his power.

Finishing the dodge. The stick remains in the box area of the opposite side until open space is gained. The player can then use either hand to pass or shoot.

Shooting

Shooting is obviously an essential part of the game. You can't score if you don't shoot. This sounds like a simple statement, but too often players are reluctant to shoot. Encourage your players to shoot. There are several types of shots they can take. Begin by teaching and reinforcing what they already know. Shooting is similar to the passing motion (see Passing, page 32). As players become more comfortable with the overhand shooting–passing motion, have them experiment with other types of shots, including the three-quarter arm, side arm, and underarm shot. Each shot can be used in different situations. (See Shooting Drills, pages 98–102.)

As the player's shoulders rotate to shoot, his eyes and lower body should face the target.

The overhand shot gives the most accuracy and makes it very difficult for the goalie to read where the shot is going. As the shot moves out of the overhand position, accuracy tends to decrease, but power usually increases. It's important that players give their shots a chance to score. The first step is to hit the goal. Step two relates to players' position on the field. For shots outside of 10 yards, players should shoot a bounce shot, aiming several feet outside the crease. On shots that are inside of 10 yards, players should focus on opposites. If the stick is in the overhand position, fake high and shoot low. It's also important for players to develop the ability to look off the shot inside of 10 yards. Otherwise, the goalie may be able to read the shot. As players are learning to shoot in close, they tend to look where they're shooting. Players should also consider the conditions of the field when shooting and select the type of shot accordingly. For example, harder ground will cause the ball to bounce high, and wet conditions will cause the ball to skid.

The stance. To begin, the player stands facing the direction in which he intends to shoot. His feet are offset. If the player is left-handed, his right foot is in front of the left. If the player is right-handed, his left foot is in front of the right. This positioning is similar to throwing a ball.

Trunk rotation. The player rotates at the waist so that his shoulders become perpendicular to the goal.

Hand position. The player's top hand is positioned near the head of his stick. The thumb of his top hand is extended up the shaft of the stick to help with accuracy. His bottom hand is located at the bottom of the stick and serves as a pivot point for the throw.

The shooting motion. The player pulls the stick back so that his top hand is positioned above the shoulder by about 6 inches. His top hand and arm push the stick forward in the direction of the box area. His bottom hand provides the power for the shot. The player's hand and arm are about 6 inches from the body and across the waist. The bottom hand acts as a hinge or pivot and moves back toward the body slightly as the top hand and arm extend forward. The speed of the action determines the speed of the shot.

Left: The player positions his feet with a stride toward the target, and the stick is extended backward.

Right: By lengthening his stride, the player increases the power of the shot.

Left: The body is rotated, with the head and legs facing the target. Trunk rotation adds power.

Right: Finishing the shot is important for accuracy and power. The head and legs are facing the target, and rotation of the shoulders is complete.

Finishing the shot. The player's top arm extends fully in the direction of the shot, which helps with accuracy. The player's front foot steps forward toward the goal. His weight shifts from the back foot to the front foot as part of the step, which helps add power to the shot. The wrist of the player's top hand moves from a normal resting position to an extended position at the end of the shot. This can be demonstrated by having a player shoot with one arm and hand.

The shooting motion is very similar to the passing motion. The difference is in the increased power of the release in the shot and the longer stride taken by the shooter.

Screening

The skill of screening is an important offensive skill and is considered something of a lost art. The idea is to utilize an offensive player playing in the area above the crease to obstruct the goalie's vision of the ball.

Screening is difficult. Here the player is allowing the shot to pass between his legs. Feet are shoulder-width apart. The stick is in the box area in case of a high bounce. The player is light on his feet, maintaining ground contact for balance but elevating to the balls of his feet to spin for a rebound.

The stance. The screening player positions himself about 2 yards off the crease. This allows the player to be close enough to the goalie, but far enough from the crease so that he doesn't step in the crease and the defender can't check him into the crease.

Body motion. The screener adjusts his position to maintain a line between the goalie and the ball.

When there's a screening player, encourage the shooter to shoot low. The screener tries to allow the ball to pass between his legs or just to the side of his legs. The screener should avoid jumping because the movement takes him out of position to turn for a rebound and because it makes him vulnerable to a body check.

Finishing the screen. The screener turns to look for a rebound once the shot has passed him.

Screeners are usually taught to choke up on the stick so that they have a quicker reaction time to gather and shoot or slap in a rebound.

Pick

The pick helps players take advantage of spaces. This is done by a teammate coming to a stationary position that blocks the pathway of a defender. Picks can occur *on the ball* or *off the ball*. On-the-ball picks help players who are under pressure to gain space and create opportunities to execute the *pick and roll*. The pick-and-roll is a two-player combination where the player who sets the pick rolls, or *cuts*, to the goal to receive a pass and shoot. Off-the-ball picks are designed to help one player, the *cutter*, move into open space to create either a *passing lane* (open spaces the cutter can move into to receive a pass) and receive a *feed*, or

Setting the pick. Feet are shoulder-width apart; the hands are a comfortable distance apart. Note the stick position in the box area. This allows the player to spin once, execute the pick, and be available to receive a pass.

pass, or to cut to open up space for another player. The difference is that the pick draws two defenders and creates space for the roll.

Face-Off

The face-off starts the action at the beginning of a game, at the beginning of each quarter or half, and after a goal has been scored. The essential part of the face-off lies with gaining possession. There are many techniques that help a player win the face-off and the team maintain or gain momentum. The face-off is as essential as the ground ball in giving teams a possession advantage.

The basic stance. A player begins a face-off by gripping the stick with his right hand at the top of the stick, even on the plastic of the head. His hand grips the stick with the palm underneath the stick facing upward and the thumb overlapping the top of the shaft. His left hand grips several inches from the end of the shaft, with the palm facing downward and the thumb wrapping underneath or along the shaft. The player squats with his feet shoulder-width apart and balances on the balls of his feet. This position

Left: The players are balanced, and the hand location and grips are proper.

Right: The player on the left is demonstrating the clamp. He has used his quickness to win the battle.

helps the player maintain balance and power and allows him to move quickly once the whistle blows. The head of the stick is placed about an inch away from the ball, with the narrow part of the head in line with the ball. The stick lightly touches the ground, with the weight of the player supported by his legs, not his hands. For the face-off, right- and left-handed players hold the stick the same way.

The clamp. This is the most basic move for winning possession. On the whistle, the player rolls his wrists toward the ball and uses the head of the stick to trap the ball underneath. Once this move is completed, the player can use a sweeping motion to pull the ball away from his opponent to one of his wing players or to open space.

The rake. Raking the ball uses a player's quickness. The player pushes his stick toward the opponent's stick as a block and uses a sweeping motion with the head of his stick to pull the ball to the side.

The punch and drag. This move involves power and finesse. The power is supplied by the punch. As with the rake, the punch pushes the stick forward, blocking the opponent's stick. The head of the stick moves over top of the ball, and the player steps, takes a wider stance with the right leg, and flips the ball between his legs to a position behind him. More advanced players are able to scoop after the punch instead of dragging the ball behind. Once players learn the basics, they'll develop other techniques and learn to counter an opponent's moves.

Defensive Position and Checks

The basic stance. The proper stance is similar to a boxer's stance. A defender stands with his feet shoulder-width apart and with one foot slightly ahead of the other in the direction the offensive player is moving. The knees are bent, and the player's weight is distributed equally on the balls of his feet. His hands are waist high and slightly extended. His back is straight and leaning slightly forward, and his head is up.

Footwork. A defensive player needs to be able to move in several specific ways. In addition to movement forward and backward, a defender needs

to do a *shuffle* and a *side sprint*. The shuffle is used to move from side to side and is the best position for checking because it allows the defender to maintain his angle and balance. The side sprint is a similar movement, but is done faster. If the attacking player in possession of the ball is moving with speed, the defender needs to move quickly to maintain position between the goal and the attacker. As the defender sprints, his shoulders remain square to the offensive player.

The stick position. The stick is used to maintain distance between the offensive player and the defender, and should be on the *stick side* of the offensive player. When the offensive player is moving with the ball under defensive pressure, he should use his shoulders and body to protect the ball by putting his stick as far away from the defender as possible. The defender wants to keep his stick on the side the offensive player is moving toward. This allows the defender to put pressure on the offensive player's stick or hands if the offensive player attempts to shoot or pass.

Left: This technique is a modification to the clamp. The player on the left adjusts his body to give protection and increase leverage to work the ball free.

Right: The player on the left is demonstrating a power and quickness move by blocking the opponent's stick and by pulling the ball free or scooping the ball to gain possession.

The player should take a comfortable stance, with his head up, his back straight, and his arms a comfortable distance apart.

The stick should also be *on the hands*, which is poke checking (see below) or lifting his bottom hand, and disrupting the offensive player's normal passing or shooting motion.

The hold position. If the defender loses his *cushion* (the space between himself and the offensive player), the hold is used to slow the defender's penetration and regain the player's cushion. The hold is executed by the defender placing his front (top) arm parallel to the ground across the middle of the attacker's back or side, forming an L with his arm and stick. The stick forces the player in one direction, and the L drives the player away from the goal. The off-hand hold is more difficult to use and gives the defender less control. Here the bottom hand of the defender is placed on the lead shoulder of the attacker and is used to drive the player back. The off-hand hold is used most often on roll dodges, where the attacker is driving in one direction and the defender is unable to switch the stick to the front of the offensive player when he rolls back.

The poke check. The defender begins in the proper stance. As the attacker penetrates, the defender places the head of his stick on the hands or hip of the attacker and drives the head of the stick forward by pushing the bottom hand on the stick forward and using the top hand as a guide. Proper position is maintained throughout the check. The player should be careful not to lunge his body forward, or he might lose his balance and position.

The slap check. The defender begins in the proper stance. As the attacker penetrates, the defender draws the stick away from the offensive player for a short distance and then brings it back toward the attacker with a quick snap of the wrists, creating a slapping motion. The slap can only cover a short distance and should hit the hands or stick. Repeated slapping motions may result in a slashing foul.

The wrap check. This check is more risky because it pulls defenders out of position. To execute the wrap check the defender must overplay to the stick side. The player extends his stick beyond the normal position and wraps the stick around the midsection of the offensive player, making contact with the stick. This check is effective for dislodging the ball because the attacker can't hide the head and shaft of the stick.

The Fundamentals of Offense

The philosophy behind playing offense is quite simple: try to score goals using dodging, passing, and shooting. Your team's success will rely on the players' ability to execute the fundamental skills, move effectively, communicate specifically, and make quality decisions. There are many different formations and strategies your team can use to create scoring opportunities. This section introduces several options and provides a basic understanding of each formation, but it's up to you to decide which one fits your team best. It's also important for individual players to understand their roles.

Offensive Players

The offense consists of three midfielders and three attackers. Midfielders are responsible for playing both offense and defense and have a responsibility to link the defense with the offense, gain and maintain possession, assist, and score. Attackers are generally limited to playing in the offensive half of the field only and are responsible for maintaining possession, assisting, and scoring.

Midfielders and attackers have three basic offensive roles: first attacker, second attacker, and third attacker. The *first attacker* is the player with the ball. It's his job to penetrate the attack area by dodging, passing, or shooting. Once this player realizes he cannot penetrate, he must possess the ball. A player develops these skills by working with the fundamental and team drills. The *second attacker* provides help for the first attacker. This is the player who's closest to the first attacker, the player in possession of the ball. Once the first attacker realizes he cannot penetrate the attack area, the second attacker needs to provide an outlet or provide help for the first attacker to gain open space. The second attacker provides support by being in the first attacker's vision and by executing a *V-cut* to gain space away from his covering defender to receive a pass. To execute a V-cut, the attacker moves into a defender or a defender's space and then explodes away into open space while moving toward the ball. The path of this motion looks like a V. The second attacker can also execute a pick on the ball to help the first attacker gain open space by blocking the pathway of the opponent who is defending the first attacker. The role of *third attacker* is the responsibility of everyone else on the team other than the first or second attacker. Third attackers are re-

Place players in practice situations that encourage decision making.

sponsible for backing up shots, setting off-the-ball picks, screening shots, and cutting. They must maintain team shape and field balance to prevent fast breaks for the other team. Through practice in drills and games, players will began to understand how all these responsibilities blend to create team offense. (See chapter 9, Offensive Drills.)

Team Formations

Team formations are used to assist your team's offensive strength. Certain formations are good for utilizing the dodge, others are used for possession, and still others support teams that move well. Learning your players strengths' and understanding the formations will help you understand which offensive formation is best for your team and which formation is best for exposing a defense's weaknesses. The following team formations are described from the positions on the field, top center to point behind (the position directly behind the goal). These descriptions are very basic and are intended to introduce the formations and how they relate to using space and movement. Many creative plays can be run from all of these formations.

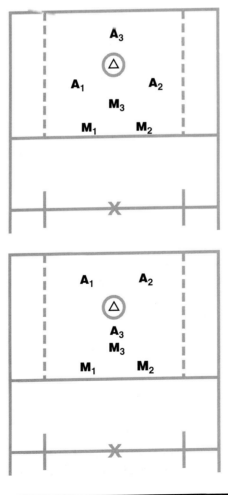

See Diagram Key, page 83. The 2-3-1 formation is a two-triangle offense, with one triangle of midfielders and one of attackers.

See Diagram Key, page 83. In 2-2-2 formations, crease players can play stacked (as shown) or side by side.

The 2-3-1 formation. This formation is a two-triangle formation. The midfielders form one triangle. Two midfielders occupy top left and top right. One midfielder occupies the crease. Two attackers play the low left and low right positions, and one attacker plays point behind. The offense supports movement with the *pass and go*, where players pass, relax, and cut to the goal. The other players balance and maintain the triangles. This is a very good motion offense and supports dodging. It is one of the best and most popular formations.

The 2-2-2 formation. This formation is set up for dodging because it creates larger spaces at top left, top right, low left, and low right. These spaces make defensive slides longer, allowing the offense more time to make decisions (for more on slides, see page 49). The formation is more difficult for teams that aren't strong dodging teams because the help players (the second and third attackers and defenders) are greater distances from the ball. This is also a good offense for teams that have quality crease players.

The 1-4-1 formation. The 1-4-1 formation is great for dodging and picking for players off the ball. Teams that are good at these skills can utilize the formation to gain high percentage shots. Inside crease players can pick for the outside wing players or each other. This offense allows for larger sweeping dodges where stronger players can use their power.

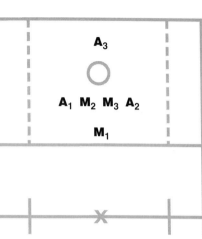

See Diagram Key, page 83. The 1-4-1 formation is great for using the pick to create high percentage shots.

The 3-2-1 circle formation. The circle formation is excellent for maintaining possession and giving the midfielders and defense a chance to rest once they've played defense for an extended period of time. The circle opens up the middle of the field for cutters and gives the first attacker close support.

See Diagram Key, page 83. The 3-2-1 circle formation is used to maintain possession and create open space in the center just above the crease.

Zone offense. A zone offense is used to combat the zone defense, which is designed to limit the offensive team's ability to dodge by having help defenders already in the help position. Players guard areas instead of players. To combat the zone defense, the offense simply needs to adjust their normal formations. Offensive teams need to focus on the fundamental skills of quick passing, effective cutting, and effective off-the-ball picks to increase their scoring opportunities. The ball moves faster than the feet. Simply moving the ball from one side of the field to the other before a team can adjust will create shooting opportunities. *Skip passes* can accomplish this, where a player skips over passing to the player next to him and instead passes the ball to the player next to the player next to him. Having players cut into and out of a zone creates passing lanes. As a defender follows one offensive player out of his area, another offensive player enters the other side of the defender's zone, making it impossible for the defender to cover that player. Picks work in a similar way. One offensive player picks and seals an area of the zone from a defender as another player moves into the open space. The success of a zone offense lies in passing and catching, vision of the zone, and movement without the ball.

Each of these formations can be successful for team offense. It's up to you to determine which one is best for your team, the defense you're facing, and the game situation you're in. It's important to develop your team offense beginning under limited pressure by the defense and then increasing the pressure to more gamelike conditions.

Special Offensive Situations

Special offensive situations include the face-off (see pages 39–40), clearing, and extra-player offense.

Clearing the ball involves the entire team in an offensive situation. The idea is to utilize your numerical advantage to create open space to move the ball from defense to offense. Clearing occurs whenever there is a change of possession in the defensive half of the field. There are settled and unsettled clearing situations. *Settled clearing* situations occur when there are stoppages of play—after a pass or shot goes out-of-bounds, after a rule infraction, or after a time-out. *Unsettled clearing* situations occur when there's a steal, loose ground ball, or save. Each has the same basic principles. First, it's important for players to recognize they're in a clearing situation. The communication should start from the goalie and be echoed by the field players.

A clearing opportunity is finished when players gain open space by running with the ball, passing to other players, and moving without the ball to open space. The first option in clearing the ball is to run. Remember that the role of the first attacker is to penetrate. There are various formations teams can use to help create opportunities for penetration. Basic formations might include lining the three defenders and the goalie across the field, with the goalie either to the left or right of the goal and the midfielders stretched three across the midfield. The numerical advantage is with the defenders and goalie. Other formations might include moving a midfielder down and switching him with a defender. This puts the ball with a player who is typically a more sure-handed player. The defender at the midfield can stay and be used to clear or can be subbed through the box for a midfielder, creating a short-stick numerical advantage. Another formation is to align midfielders on one side of the field and attempt to clear up an alley or side. This opens the middle of the field and forces the defensive team to make decisions on how to defend. There is no right or wrong way to clear the ball. The important factor is to space the players effectively and focus on off-the-ball movement and vision of the field. Remember that the player who is open is usually the player farthest from the ball. It's important to practice these long passes in order to make clearing effective.

Another special offensive situation is *extra-player offense*. This occurs when the defensive team is assessed a penalty, giving the offensive team a numerical advantage and a greater chance for scoring. When the penalty is called, the offensive team is awarded the ball in the offensive half of the field and has a one-player advantage. Additional penalties by different players would result in an additional numerical advantage. Additional penalties by the same player would result in additional time for the one-player advantage.

How you take advantage of this extra player is crucial. There is no need to deviate from any of your normal offensive formations. What is important is to create a *set play* that will give your team the best shot possible. Set plays utilize a prescribed pattern of movement by your players. Players move to overload an area, or to clear an area, and make it difficult for the defense to defend against your numerical advantage, or the open space. Teams find it easy to learn extra-player offense by practicing cutting and picking and by having players move from one offensive formation to another. This switch in formation is effective because the defensive team needs time to recognize the new formation and to change the shape of their zone defense. Also, it's extremely important to pass the ball quickly during the extra-player offense to beat the defense.

Fundamentals of Defense

If the goal of team offense is scoring, the obvious goal of team defense is preventing the other team from scoring. To play successful team defense you need to develop a system that works for your team, and your players need to play good fundamental individual defense. (See chapter 10, Defensive Drills.)

In order to be successful as a team on defense your players need to limit the space in which the opposing offense can operate, limit the time the offense has to make decisions, and limit penetration by the offensive players. These three rules apply to individuals and the team as a whole. Begin teaching team defense by defining defensive roles and by discussing the fundamentals of defense.

Defensive Players

The *first defender* is the player defending the opponent in possession of the ball, the first attacker. The first defender's role is to prevent penetration by the first attacker, and there are three important steps in doing so. The first defender must approach the first attacker with speed by moving into position as quickly as possible. He also approaches at an angle, which forces the attacker to one side and limits the space he has to attack. Finally, the first defender must maintain a proper distance, or cushion, from the first attacker. The optimal distance is about a half to a full stick length away. This still allows the defender to apply pressure on the hands of the first attacker while allowing space to adjust to the offensive player's dodges. If the first defender is too far away, he's vulnerable to penetration by a dodge. If the defender is too close, he's vulnerable to penetration by a pass or shot.

Failure to break down into a proper defensive position also creates problems for the defender. Encourage your players to assume a boxer's stance, with knees bent, weight on the balls of the feet, arms slightly extended with the stick on the stick side of the offensive player, and head up.

The *second defender* provides help for the first defender. This is the player who slides to help if the first defender is dodged to the goal. Communication by the second defender is important so that the first defender is aware of the angle of his help. The second defender needs to be in a help position, where he covers the next closest offensive player, is able to slide if needed, and occupies a passing lane. There is a general rule in defending off the ball that says defenders should watch both the player they're marking and the ball. Watching the ball allows the defender to adjust his defense according to the location of the ball. The off-the-ball defensive player should form a triangle between the player with the ball, the player he's covering, and himself. This usually will put the defender in good help positions while still being able to see the player he's covering. This is true until the player being marked moves to a dangerous scoring position. That puts increased pressure on the defense and requires defenders to tighten up, concentrating more on the player they're defending.

The *third defender* covers the next most dangerous players and occupies passing lanes. Third defenders are all of the other defenders who are not marking the player in possession of the ball and who are not the closest teammate to the player marking the player with the ball. It's important for the third defenders to recognize the second defender slide so that the next closest defender can make the second slide to a help position. In this situation all other defenders must move into helping positions by either marking tighter or covering the hole (the crease area in front of the goal).

The final piece of the puzzle for individual defense is the *goalie*, the "quarterback" of the defense and of the team. The goalie's primary role is to prevent the ball from going into the goal, a role that extends to all aspects of the game. The goalie leads the defense. He's responsible for calling out the ball's position on the field, such as top right or left behind. He's the leader on the clear, communicating the clear and executing the clear pass if needed. The goalie must be aware of the type of defense being played, all defensive roles, and the communication to his players about who's in those roles at all times. Once the play moves to the offensive end of the field, the goalie is responsible for making sure the defense is alert to the potential for fast breaks and continues to communicate with the offense because he has better vision of the entire field and of the coaching area. Just like the quarterback in football, the goalie calls all the plays.

Slides

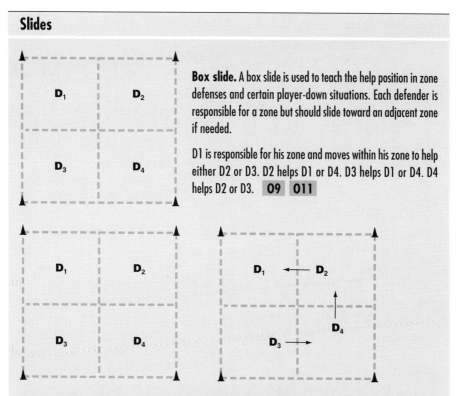

Box slide. A box slide is used to teach the help position in zone defenses and certain player-down situations. Each defender is responsible for a zone but should slide toward an adjacent zone if needed.

D1 is responsible for his zone and moves within his zone to help either D2 or D3. D2 helps D1 or D4. D3 helps D1 or D4. D4 helps D2 or D3. **O9** **O11**

Rotation slide. A rotation slide is used in zone defense, player-to-player defense, and player-down defense. Players are responsible for their zone but rotate (slide) to help an adjacent player if needed. Once a player slides, all the players follow—as if connected by a string—and are pulled to the next zone. **O9** **O11**

If D1 is defending and needs help, D2 slides to help (if he is the closest defender). D4 then slides to D2's zone and D3 slides across to fill D4's zone.

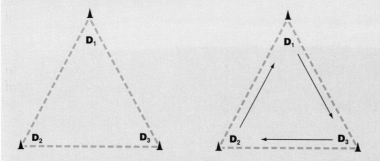

Triangle slide. The triangle slide is a rotation slide that is part of a six-on-six defense. Players rotate (slide) to help as needed and replace each other. Triangle slides are used in the drills to emphasize the roles of the first, second, and third defenders. **F24** **O5** **O11** **D10**

Stack slide. A stack slide is a two-player combination where D1 moves to the ball and D2 guards the hole, the area in front of the goal. On the next pass, D2 moves to the ball and D1 recovers to the hole. **O8** **D5**

Team Formations

Team defense involves a group of players collectively working to prevent the opponent from scoring. When a team is on the defense, there's an extra player—the goalie—to help. What becomes difficult about team defense is the coordination of those players. If you've successfully worked on the roles of the defenders with your players, you have a clear advantage. Communication then becomes the link that will help your team. Once the individual roles are clearly defined and understood, execution is the only part left. Teams can elect to play player-to-player defense or zone defense.

Player-to-player defense. The basic concept behind player-to-player defense is that every player is responsible for a player on the opposing team. Success lies in the ability of the first defender to stop the first attacker, and the ability of the team to adjust if the player is unable to stop the first attacker. In player-to-player defense the defenders should always work to keep their position *ball-side* (between the opponent and the ball) and *goal-side* (between the opponent and the goal) of the offensive players they are covering. By doing this, they prevent an open passing lane and an open path to the goal. As the ball moves around the perimeter of the offensive zone, it's important for the defenders to recognize that their roles change. In teaching this concept, progress slowly with perimeter passing and then move to game-like conditions.

Zone defense. A zone defense is designed to cover areas and opposing players who move into a defender's area. One of the strengths of zone defense is that the second defender is usually predetermined and is not altered by the movement of the offensive players. Zones typically force shots from the outside when well played. A team that has a quality goalie may use zone defense to their advantage. The difficult part of playing the zone occurs when more than one player is in an area, and help is needed off the ball.

If necessary, take a player's place to demonstrate a move or technique.

The roles remain the same in the zone as they do for player-to-player defense. Although there are many modifications that can be made to zones, they are typically more passive and not as useful as player-to-player defense for placing pressure on offenses or for obtaining possession when trailing late in a game. Zones are very effective in special situations, such as coming out of time-outs, because they often disrupt the normal offense of the opponent by giving them a different defense to work against.

Special Defensive Situations

One special defensive situation is the *player-down defense*. When one team commits a penalty, that team must play without one defender. Understanding the fundamentals of defense is essential to playing successful player-down defense. Usually a team plays with three defenders and two midfielders in a player-down situation. One of the midfielders typically uses a defensive stick. When your players are in a player-down defense, encourage them to shift toward the ball and leave the player farthest from the ball open.

There are two ways to play player-down defense. Your defensive team can rotate positions, moving around the perimeter and low positions on each pass, executing box slides, and allowing the crease player to remain in position, or you can maintain a standard 2-1-2 formation, with players extending to the ball when it's in their area and collapsing toward the crease when the ball is away. Experiment with the system that works best for your team. The player-down defense is also a good opportunity to get good athletic players who may not have great offensive stick skills into the game.

Riding is another special defensive situation. Riding begins with the attackers and their role as defenders. The ride involves trying to slow the opponent from transitioning from defense to offense and trying to create a turnover to regain possession. Riding requires heart and hustle. By using the fundamentals of defense, your team can create many unsettled situations and good scoring opportunities.

There are several types of rides that a team can use. One style, the *ten-player ride*, places pressure all over the field. The ten-player ride involves the goalie marking an opposing attacker (usually the one farthest away from where the ball begins), the defenders marking the remaining attackers and one midfielder, the midfielders defending the remaining midfielders and one defender, and the attackers defending the goalie and the two remaining defenders. All opposing players are marked, and the key is to prevent penetration while positioning the defender between the player with the ball and the goal. Other defenders can't allow an opposing player any space behind them and must be close enough to defend immediately or intercept a pass.

Other styles of riding place less immediate pressure on the opponent but instead *trap* at specific areas of the field. A trap is executed by forcing a player into a closed space, a space where there are multiple defenders, or where offensive options are limited by field boundaries. The attackers can play as a triangle, with one point player forcing a pass to the outside of the field, where he can chase and trap with one of the other attackers. The midfielders play three across the midfield in this situation and don't allow anyone behind them. Defenders cover the opposing attackers.

Other rides might move the attack outside the restraining line and place the defenders in a three-across role like the midfielders, not allowing anyone behind them, forcing the ball to one side, and using the sideline as a trap. There are many ways to ride. Keep in mind that what works best is whatever is best at slowing down the other team. If your team is very athletic, try using a ride with more pressure. If your team is slower, have them drop back and shorten up the field. Trying different formations will help confuse the clearing team, but find a style that fits your team and encourage heart and hustle.

CHAPTER 5

The Practice

Preparation Is the Key

Make a point of coming to practice with a written plan of exactly what you and your players will do. With so much going on at once, even seasoned coaches need a written reminder of what's going on next. Don't feel that having a written plan is a reflection of your poor memory; instead, think of it as an indication of your excellent organizational abilities!

Before arriving at practice, write a practice plan using as a guideline the goals and objectives that you, your players, and their parents created at the preseason meeting. As the season progresses, these objectives may have to be adjusted slightly to address newly emerging needs. Design a practice plan that lets players experience maximum movement with gamelike activities that require problem solving, and that stretches their abilities while maintaining a safe, flexible, fun environment. What separates good practices from really good practices are the numbers of activities that require problem solving and promote creativity. Many of these activities may be introduced using a small-sided format. Having your players practice in small groups increases their participation and provides opportunities for hundreds of chances with the ball. It allows them to focus on a particular dimension of the game without concern for all of the other parts. As you plan the practice, remember to keep your demonstration brief and to the point. This helps reduce the periods of inactivity for the players. (But make sure that players understand the drill; a visual demonstration often helps.) Small groups of players can work on the same skill with the same drill, or groups with varying abilities can work on the same skill but use different drills that are better suited to their needs. We recommend using one or more assistant coaches to work with different groups in a *station format*, where small groups of players rotate to different *stations* (areas of the field) as different skills are being presented. Players generally spend 10 to 15 minutes at each station before rotating. Having station work in a small-sided format means more skills can be presented in less time. Players have the chance to improve skills more quickly because they have more repetitions.

When you plan out your practices, plan for activity-filled sessions, but remember to schedule frequent water and bathroom breaks.

Arrive Early

Try to arrive at the practice site at least 20 minutes before the players. Make it clear to parents that no player should be dropped off and left unattended until you arrive. You can use these extra 20 minutes to review your practice plan and set up the field for practice. This may include positioning goals, putting nets on goals, placing *field markers* (rubber cones) to identify *grids* (spaces) for station work, and checking the field to ensure it's free from debris.

Start on Time

Always try to start practice exactly when it's scheduled to start so players get used to a routine. This helps promote a positive environment. Don't forget the hustle contract that you and your players agreed to at your preseason meeting (see page 8). Carry out your part by being ready to start right on time and showing your players you expect them to fulfill their side of the bargain.

When it's time for practice to begin, go to the spot on the field that you've decided is the best place for a huddle. Signal the players with your call to huddle—we use two strong whistle blasts. Give your players 10 seconds to get to the huddle spot, and remind them that if they don't show enough hustle, you earn 1 point (see pages 8–9).

Explain to your players exactly what they'll be doing at each practice. At least for the first couple of practices, this is a good time to reinforce the player expectations discussed at the preseason meeting (see pages 6–7). This is also a good time to encourage dialogue with your players. See if they have any questions for you, and ask them some questions as well. If a player is obviously stuck and can't answer a question, allow him to "pass" to another player. This helps avoid embarrassing players in front of their peer group and lets them know you're not trying to pull any "I gotchas." The dialogue helps form a bond of trust and open lines of communication between you and your players. The huddle is also a good time to remind players of safety concerns. Establishing good safety habits (such as always wearing a helmet when doing anything on the practice field) and adherence to team expectations early in the season helps cultivate an atmosphere for learning.

For the first few practices, while you're talking to the players, occasionally hold your hand out and shake one of the player's hands. If you don't know the player's name, shake his hand and say, "Hi, I'm Coach [name], what's your name?" Then go on with your brief review for the day. The players will like the personal contact, and you'll learn their names

Safety Concerns

Along with making sure your players have fun, you need to ensure their safety. Before practices or games, check the field to make sure it is free of potential hazards such as holes in the ground or debris like broken glass. Be sure the goals are not broken.

Players should have a designated area to put on equipment. It's a good idea to have an assistant coach or a parent volunteer in charge of this area. They can check to see that players are wearing the proper equipment and have put it on correctly. Be sure players know that they must be wearing the proper equipment before any ball playing is allowed (although no ball playing should ever be allowed in this area). This is a good time to check that players are wearing NOCSAE-approved helmets, and that the helmet screws are tight.

Once all the players are ready, begin the practice with your huddle and then the warm-up. During the warm-up, players should have enough space to move around in without contacting other players. Teach your players to be aware of the space around them so they avoid unnecessary contact.

Early training sessions with beginning players should include teaching them how to move safely and efficiently through *open* (unoccupied) spaces while avoiding *closed* (occupied) spaces (see drills F1–F4, pages 84–86). Of course, contact is part of the game of lacrosse, but your players will learn the appropriate ways to initiate contact as they progress.

Be sure all the players know to "play the whistle": play begins with one whistle blast and stops immediately on one whistle blast.

faster. Once you know everyone's name, change the dialogue slightly. Reach out, shake a player's hand, and say something like, "Hi, John, good to see you today."

Practice Format and Sample Practices

Establishing a practice routine is important for you and the players. It helps you provide structure for the practice environment and helps players establish good practice habits and know what to expect next. You can follow the same basic routine for each practice but vary the activities, number of players, player combinations, space, and concepts presented to keep players motivated. A practice worksheet, like those shown on pages 56 and 57, is an excellent planning tool. This worksheet is for a 70-minute practice with beginning players. You can adjust the times for the individual segments to fit your time schedule and your team's needs.

In the remainder of this chapter we outline three sample practices. The examples provided show a beginning, intermediate, and advanced practice. Each practice is designed in the same format, although the skills and concepts are modified to meet the needs of each level. First is the amount of practice time. Beginning practices (for 6- to 8-year-old players) should last 45 to 60 minutes. Intermediate practices (for 9- to 10-year-old players) should last from 60 to 75 minutes. Advanced practices (for 11- to 13-year-old players) should last between 75 minutes and 2 hours.

Practice Session Worksheet

Team huddle (5 min.):

_____
_____
_____

Warm-up (10 min.):

_____
_____
_____

Stretching (5 min.):

_____
_____
_____

Fundamentals (20 min.):

_____
_____
_____

Offense-defense combinations (10 min.):

_____
_____
_____

Ending activity (10 min.):

_____
_____
_____

Cooldown/stretch (5 min.):

_____
_____
_____

Wrap-up/huddle (5 min.):

_____
_____
_____
_____

Practice Session Worksheet

Team huddle (5 min.):
Welcome.
Discuss purpose of today's practice: moving in open spaces, recognition of open space, creating open space.

Warm-up (10 min.):
Grid tag: recognition of open space, exploding into open space.

Stretching (5 min.):
Stretch legs and neck.

Fundamentals (20 min.):
Four-Corner Hot Potato: explode to open marker (space), work to give two adjacent passing options.

Offense-defense combinations (10 min.):
Goalie Game and Four-on-Three Defensive Possession: creating open space with communication and off-ball movement (lateral and diagonal runs).

Ending activity (10 min.):
Half-field scrimmage: stop play to point out good movement and to show players where a specific run might create an opportunity for themselves or a teammate.

Cooldown/stretch (5 min.):
Talk with each player about something related to movement that he did well.

Wrap-up/huddle (5 min.):
Review each drill and have a few players assess the practice.

Second, each sample practice uses drills that are developmentally appropriate. When you design practices, remember to choose drills with age and ability in mind. They should also follow an appropriate progression. Begin with fundamental drills (chapter 8) before expecting players to execute team offensive drills (chapter 9) and defensive drills (chapter 10). The fundamental drills address basic principles and break the team drills into smaller segments.

Modifications of drills involving time and space are important as you progress from beginning to intermediate to advanced practices. You can modify the time a player has to make a decision with the ball by changing the number of steps a player can take with the ball, by adding additional offensive players or defenders, or by limiting the number of cradles a player can take. Space can be limited by making the grid smaller, by adding offensive or defensive pressure, or by restricting a player to a certain area. These modifications all challenge the players' decision making by requiring them to make quicker decisions and by increasing the number of decisions they need to make.

The following is a sample practice that works on maintaining possession. Notice that the format remains the same for the beginning, intermediate, and advanced levels. The drills selected in this sample are identical, but we've modified them to meet the developmental needs of the players involved for each level. Although we've chosen to use the same drills for each level by modifying them, you can also select different drills for each level of play. We chose the same drills on purpose to demonstrate how coaches can modify drills to become age and player appropriate. To plan practices for your team that address different needs, use this format and refer to the fundamental drills (chapter 8), the offensive drills (chapter 9), and the defensive drills (chapter 10) to select drills that will be appropriate. Substitute your own drills to create a great practice that meets the needs of your team.

Beginning Practice

Team Huddle (5 minutes)

Start your practice by hustling to the spot you've selected for the team huddle and by blowing two strong whistle blasts, or by using another distinctive signal. Explain the skill or skills this practice will concentrate on to your players and discuss player expectations. Go over the importance of staying well hydrated and remind players to drink water during the scheduled breaks.

Read through the roster and determine which players are at practice. If you have specific goals for a player, it's important that you communicate this before practice starts. Ask about the status of any injuries that a player may have received from a previous game or practice or from another activity.

There's no need to discuss every drill with the team at this point. What

Use the huddle to discuss team goals or goals for smaller groups of players.

you want to emphasize here are the theme of the practice and the purpose of the warm-up activity.

Warm-Up (10 minutes)

Players at all levels need to prepare their bodies to play. Warm-up activities should be designed to build interest and enthusiasm for the practice. They are implemented with safety as the number-one priority. Activities should be appropriate for the players' age and development and should create an environment where every player can have success.

- **Grid Tag.** The game of tag is basic to the concepts of open and closed space, vision, and communication. All players need to develop an understanding of these principles in order to be successful at field sports and maintaining possession. **F1**

Stretching (5 minutes)

Stretching is essential for all players, but for different reasons. Younger players probably need to stretch less than older players simply because they don't yet have the muscle mass of the older players. Include stretches for the legs, trunk, arms, shoulders, and neck. Consult a doctor, athletic trainer, or other appropriate resource to determine what stretches your players should be doing. The period of stretching allows players to connect as a team. This is a great opportunity to have players assume a leadership role. You might have less assertive players lead the stretches, and this is a great way to involve less skilled players in important team activities. Stress the importance of the stretching part of the practice with your team.

Fundamentals (20 minutes)

Every player, no matter what level, needs to work on fundamentals. The drills in chapter 8 provide the basis for being successful in gamelike situations and in games. Take the opportunity to teach and make corrections as the players work. The drills are designed for repetition and a great deal of movement. These drills are conducted using stations, and there should be several drills occurring at the same time. No players should be standing around waiting for their turn. The tempo of these fundamental drills should be as fast-paced as is appropriate for the skill level of your players: fast enough to challenge your players while encouraging learning and success.

- **Four-Corner Hot Potato.** Players work in a 15-by-15-yard grid. The three offensive players located at the markers work to pass the ball to a player in open space. One defender tries to intercept the pass and put pressure on the offensive player with the ball. Offensive players must move to the open marker so that the player with the ball has two adjacent passes. **F7**

Offense-Defense Combinations (10 minutes)

This portion of practice is conducted using stations, so you'll need at least one assistant. One coach should work with each group. Each coach emphasizes a different skill as part of the day's theme. By approaching a practice in this way, one coach can stress offensive skills related to possession (throwing and catching), and the other coach can emphasize a different skill with defenders related to possession, such as movement without the ball, since defenders need to know how to keep possession of the ball for clearing.

- **Goalie Game.** The objective of this drill is for players to move the ball from one end of the grid to the other by utilizing their teammates and the neutral players on the side of the grid. The grid is 40 yards long by 20 yards wide. Players score when they successfully pass from one goalie to the other. If this is accomplished, the team maintains possession. For the beginning practice, you can add a neutral player to the inside of the grid. This player only plays offensively. **O6**

- **Four-on-Three Defensive Possession.** The defensive team plays in a 30-by-30-yard grid and works to keep possession. Players are not limited to a marker but can move throughout the grid. The goalie should take part in the drill. Long-stick defensive players and goalies should be on the four-player team. It may be necessary to start with only two riding players. Players can use the restraining box as the boundary. **D8**

Ending Activity (10 minutes)

Finish the practice with a half-field or full-field game. Emphasize possession of the ball. Stop play in the first 5 minutes to help connect the drills to the

Water Breaks

Break time is essential when youngsters are active. The amount of time used for breaks and the number of breaks will depend on the intensity of the activities and climate conditions. Whenever you're practicing in warm weather, take more breaks and encourage the players to replace lost fluids by drinking plenty of water. Remember that young players' bodies overheat faster than adults' do, so the duration of activities should be designed accordingly.

Remember to give your players time for bathroom breaks as well.

game. Help players with their decision making as it relates to possession. To assist possession, one team at each end of the field can be given a numerical advantage.

Cooldown/Stretch (5 minutes)

Have players meet as a group to do some postexercise stretches as a cooldown. Players can all do the same stretches or they can do different stretches, depending on their individual needs. This is also a good time to talk with individual players about the practice.

Wrap-Up/Huddle (5 minutes)

This is the part of the practice when you review and assess what your players have accomplished. Start by asking a player to tell the group what he liked best about practice and what he would like changed. To get a feel for the players' opinion about a particular drill or activity, ask for a thumbs-up if they like it, a thumbs-sideways if it was just OK, and a thumbs-down if they didn't like it. You can quickly scan the group and get an idea of how that particular drill or activity was received. It isn't necessary and would be too time consuming to ask each player to assess the practice. Pick two or three players at each practice, and be sure to pick a different set of players at the next practice. After these players have a turn to assess the practice, give players your assessment of the session. Always start out with something positive, such as, "I really liked the way you guys hustled in your station work tonight." Add some constructive criticism in an area that could use some improvement, and conclude practice by letting players know what they'll be doing at the next practice. Before dismissing players, make any other team announcements, such as fund-raising information. Lead a team cheer and then dismiss players.

Intermediate Practice

Team Huddle (5 minutes)

The objectives and procedures of the team huddle here are the same as for the beginning practice. Start by calling players to the huddle by blowing two strong whistle blasts, or by using another distinctive signal. Your explanation of the theme for the day or the beginning portion of the practice can be more elaborate than in the beginning practice. This is important to help players begin to understand their roles in greater detail and to understand how their actions relate to individual and team concepts.

This practice will run 90 minutes, but note that only 70 minutes are spent in activities and drills. The other 20 minutes are for breaks.

Warm-Up (10 minutes)

Players at all levels need to prepare their bodies to play. Warm-up activities should be designed to build interest and enthusiasm for the practice. These basic premises remain the same for all players. At the beginning level, the speed of the drill should be slow as players learn their roles and the routine. As you progress to the intermediate level, pay special attention to the speed of the activity. Remember it's a warm-up activity. Players should not go at full speed until their bodies are properly warmed and stretched.

- **Grid Tag.** The game of tag is basic to the concepts of open and closed space, vision, and communication. All players need to develop an understanding of these principles in order to be successful at field sports and maintaining possession. **F1**
  Modifications: Decrease the size of the grid. This will limit the space in which players can move. Make the game more difficult by starting with more defenders and adding defenders. This will force players to improve the quality of their movements in order to be successful.

Stretching (10 minutes)

Stretching is essential for all players, but for different reasons. Younger players probably need to stretch less than older players simply because they don't yet have the muscle mass of the older players. Include stretches for the legs, trunk, arms, shoulders, and neck. Consult a doctor, athletic trainer, or appropriate resource to determine what stretches your players should be doing. The period of stretching allows players to connect as a team. This is a great opportunity to have players assume a leadership role. You might have less assertive players lead the stretches, and this is a great way to involve less skilled players in important team activities. Stress the importance of the stretching part of the practice with your team.

Plan to extend the time for the stretching. Intermediate-level players are on average more physically mature and have greater muscle mass than beginning players, so you need to allow more stretching time.

Fundamentals (20 minutes)

Every player, no matter what level, needs to work on fundamentals. The drills in chapter 8 provide the basis for being successful in gamelike situations and in games. Take the opportunity to teach and make corrections as the players work. The tempo of these drills should be fast-paced.

Modifications can occur for all drills in several areas. The size of the spaces in which players work, the speed at which drills are executed, the amount of offensive or defensive pressure that the players receive, and the time players have to make decisions can all be modified to challenge players and to make the drill appropriate for your team. The tempo of fundamental skills should also be fast.

- **Four-Corner Hot Potato.** Players work in a 15-by-15-yard grid. The three offensive players located at the markers work to pass the ball to a player in open space. One defender tries to intercept the pass and put pressure on the offensive player with the ball. Offensive players must move to the open marker so that the player with the ball has two adjacent passes. **F7**
  Modifications: Use two defenders in the grid to challenge their decision-making skills. One player defends the offensive player with the ball while the other defender defends one of the other two offensive players. The player with the ball must decide quickly which offensive player is not defended and pass to him.

Offense-Defense Combinations (20 minutes)

This portion of practice is conducted using stations, so you'll need at least one assistant. One coach should work with each group. Each coach emphasizes a different skill as part of the day's theme. By approaching a practice in this way, one coach can stress offensive skills related to possession (throwing and catching), and the other coach can emphasize a different skill with defenders related to possession, such as movement without the ball, since defenders need to know how to keep possession of the ball for clearing.

- **Goalie Game.** The objective of this drill is for players to move the ball from one end of the grid to the other by utilizing their teammates and the neutral players on the side of the grid. The grid is 40 yards long by 20 yards wide. Players score when they successfully pass from one goalie to the other. If this is accomplished, the team maintains possession. For the intermediate practice, you can add a neutral player to the inside of the grid. This player only plays offensively. **O6**
  Modifications: Eliminate the neutral players on the side or the neutral player in the middle, but don't do both. Adjust the dimensions of the grid; try a 30-by-20 yard grid.

- **Four-on-Three Defensive Possession.** The defensive team plays in a 30-by-30-yard grid and works to keep possession. Players are not limited to a marker but can move throughout the grid. The goalie should take part in the drill. Long-stick defensive players and goalies should be on the four-player team. **D8**

Modifications: Adjust the dimensions of the grid. Make it a 40-by-20-yard grid. Narrowing the grid simulates the space between the restraining line and midfield. This space is used to maintain possession when a team has moved their attackers near midfield in a soft-pressure ride. The defensive team has all the time it needs to maintain possession, while waiting for an attacker or midfielder to break to an open area. Begin with two defenders as in the beginning drill and then add the third.

Ending Activity (20 minutes)

Finish the practice with a half-field or full-field game. Emphasize possession of the ball. Stop play in the first 5 minutes to help connect the drills to the game. Help players with their decision making as it relates to possession. To assist possession, one team at each end of the field can be given a numerical advantage.

Cooldown/Stretch (5 minutes)

Have players meet as a group to do some postexercise stretches as a cooldown. Players can all do the same stretches or they can do different stretches, depending on their individual needs. This is also a good time to talk with individual players about the practice.

Wrap-Up/Huddle (5 minutes)

Meet as a group and ask players a question related to what they did during practice. "What did we do well as a team to help us maintain possession?" Expect and foster more detailed responses from the intermediate group. Players should discuss movement, vision and scanning, communication, ball movement, and decision making. Remind players about upcoming practices and games. Ask players if anyone has an injury that needs to be evaluated. Lead a team cheer and then dismiss players.

Advanced Practice

Team Huddle (5 minutes)

The objectives and procedures of the team huddle are the same here as in the beginning practice. Start by calling players to the huddle by blowing two strong whistle blasts, or by using another distinctive signal. Explain the theme of the practice to your players and discuss player expectations. Make it very specific. Advanced players need and can accept the challenge.

This practice will run 100–110 minutes, but note that only 65–70 minutes are spent in activities and drills. The other 35–40 minutes are for breaks and discussion.

Warm-Up (10 minutes)

The warm-up should set the tone of practice. Players should work to prepare themselves for what is to come. Advanced players need to warm-up more thoroughly and completely since they'll be executing drills at a higher rate of speed, and their potential for contact in drills is greater.

- **Grid Tag.** The game of tag is basic to the concepts of open and closed space, vision, and communication. All players need to develop an understanding of these principles in order to be successful at field sports and maintaining possession. **F1**
  Modifications: Decrease the size of the grid. This will limit the space in which players can move. Make the game more difficult by starting with more defenders and adding defenders. This will force players to improve the quality of their movement in order to be successful. Give players a pattern of movement to execute. For example, have them move laterally, then diagonally, then backward, and then any direction they choose. This will challenge players by forcing them to decide how long and fast to make their runs.

Stretching (10 minutes)

Advanced players need to stretch more thoroughly and completely since they'll be executing drills at a higher rate of speed, and their potential for contact in drills is greater. Include stretches for the legs, trunk, arms, shoulders, and neck. Consult a doctor, athletic trainer, or appropriate resource to determine what stretches your players should be doing. Stress the importance of the stretching part of the practice with your team.

Fundamentals (20 minutes)

At the advanced level, your focus should be on the subtleties of the game. Pay close attention to detail, and teach your players advanced techniques. Modifications can occur for all drills in several areas. The size of the spaces in which players work, the speed at which drills are executed, the amount of pressure, offensive or defensive, that the player receives, and the time a player has to make a decision can all be modified to challenge players and to make the drill appropriate for your team.

- **Four-Corner Hot Potato.** Players work in a 15-by-15-yard grid. The three offensive players located at the markers work to pass the ball to a player in open space. One defender tries to intercept the pass and put pressure on the offensive player with the ball. Offensive players must move to the open marker so that the player with the ball has two adjacent passes. **F7**
  Modifications: Adjust the grid to 10-by-10 yards. Use two defenders in the grid. Make both these modifications for the advanced players.

Offense-Defense Combinations (20–30 minutes)

This portion of practice is conducted using stations, so you'll need at least one assistant. One coach should work with each group. Each coach emphasizes a different skill as part of the day's theme. By approaching a practice in this way, one coach can stress offensive skills related to possession (throwing and catching), and the other coach can emphasize a different skill with defenders related to possession, such as movement without the ball, since defenders need to know how to keep possession of the ball for clearing.

- **Goalie Game.** The objective of this drill is for players to move the ball from one end of the grid to the other by utilizing their teammates and the neutral players on the side of the grid. Adjust the grid to 30 yards long by 20 yards wide. Players score when they successfully pass from one goalie to the other. If this is accomplished, the team maintains possession. For the advanced practice, you can add a neutral player to the inside of the grid. This player only plays offensively. **O6**
Modifications: Eliminate the neutral players on the side and the neutral player in the middle.

- **Four-on-Three Defensive Possession.** The defensive team plays in a 30-by-30-yard grid and works to keep possession. Players are not limited to a marker but can move throughout the grid. The goalie should take part in the drill. Long-stick players should be on the four-player team. **D8**
Modifications: Adjust the dimensions of the grid. Make the grid 40 yards by 20 yards. Narrowing the grid simulates the space between the restraining line and midfield. This space is used to maintain possession when a team has moved their attackers near midfield in a soft-pressure ride. The defensive team has all the time it needs to maintain possession, while waiting for an attacker or midfielder to break to an open area. Begin with three defenders and add a fourth.

Ending Activity (25 minutes)

Finish the practice with a half-field or full-field game. Emphasize possession of the ball. Stop play in the first 5 minutes to help connect the drills to the game. Help players with their decision making as it relates to possession. To assist possession, one team at each end of the field can be given a numerical advantage.

Cooldown/Stretch (5 minutes)

Have players meet as a group to do some postexercise stretches as a cooldown. Players can all do the same stretches or they can do different stretches, depending on their individual needs. This is also a good time to talk with individual players about the practice.

Wrap-Up/Huddle (5 minutes)

Meet as a group and ask players a question related to what they did during practice. "What did we do well as a team to help us maintain possession?" Expect and foster more detailed responses from the advanced group. Players should discuss movement, vision and scanning, communication, ball movement, and decision making. Remind players about upcoming practices and games. Ask players if anyone has an injury that needs to be evaluated. Lead a team cheer and then dismiss players.

CHAPTER 6

The Game

There's nothing like opening night, so welcome to the stage, and, oh yeah, break a leg! The anticipation for the players, coaches, and parents never seems to change, no matter if it's the first game or the tenth. The moment makes some sick to their stomachs, others become very subdued, and still others seem to find endless energy. No matter how you feel, it's important to handle the situation in a calm, cool, and collected manner. If you can function in this manner, so will your players, and all the hard work from practice will shine through the excitement.

What to Expect

As a coach, you already know the outcome of the game: one team will win, and one team will lose. It's important to emphasize this to your players. When they look at the game in this way, they'll be able to accept either outcome, handle themselves with class, and feel proud of the way the team performed. You can help your team in this regard through your actions before, during, and after the game. Explain to your players that you don't base success on wins and losses but on how well they demonstrate their understanding of what was covered in practice, the effort they put into the game, and the sportsmanship they display.

Overview of the Game

Before the Game

Allow your team and the parents to see what you expect of them through your actions. Begin by meeting the officials before the game begins. Welcome them to your field, and make sure they have what they need. Respect the tough job they have. Welcome the opposing team, introduce yourself to the coach, and make sure they have what they need. These actions are not

Lacrosse Officials

The role of officials is to enforce the rules of the game while maintaining the safety of the players. The number of officials varies from league to league, but at least two officials are required.

All officials on the field have the authority to call violations and fouls as they occur. Their specific roles change slightly depending on their position on the field in relation to the ball. The official closest to the ball focuses on the ball and the players involved directly in the play. The trailing official(s) monitor the midfield line in transition and watch the off-ball play. Common referee signals are shown on pages 128–29.

If you disagree with an official's call, don't dwell on it. You and your players need to move on and concentrate on the next play and the game situation. Remember that you're supposed to be providing a positive role model for your players, and if you let a bad call affect you, your team will notice and be adversely affected as well. Remind them (and yourself) that your team and individual goals include good sportsmanship and mutual respect.

just part of being polite; they show respect for the game and will help your parents and players begin to build respect for the game.

Game Time

You've spent a lot of time preparing for practices and you'll need to do the same for games. Your plan should include what time to arrive and what pregame details need to be completed. Who's going to complete what tasks? What time should your team arrive, and what procedures should they follow? Your players should know in advance what positions they will play, what is expected of them, and how substitutions will occur (see pages 70–71). This allows them to do their jobs more effectively and eliminates questions during the game, which might distract them and you. Once the game begins, how will you handle a player injury, a poor call by an official, a question about something that has occurred, a large goal lead, a large goal deficit, a small lead, or a small goal deficit? Having a plan and role-playing in advance will help you be successful.

After the Game

When the game is over, end as you began. Thank the officials for their work, shake the opposing coach's hand, and have your team shake the other team's hands; demonstrate the classy actions you want your players to emulate. Then gather your team together as a group, and begin to discuss the team's performance. Keep it short and specific. Address the goals and objectives you and your players discussed before the game. Players will be anxious to get home, and parents will want to discuss the game with their kids. Talk about things the players did as a team, and then ask the players what they feel they did well as a team and what they need to focus on in order to improve their performance. Win or lose, keep it positive.

Save the specific points of the game for the next practice. This will allow players a chance to reflect on the game and will give you a chance to make a list of weak and strong areas. You'll be able to change or enhance their actions through planning and purposeful drills at the next practice.

Handling Specific Game Situations

Player Substitution

This issue can make or break a coach. How and when you substitute players affects both parents and kids and can complicate the game itself if you don't have a plan to follow that's fair and one that players and parents understand. Substitution is an issue that might be discussed at the preseason parent meeting so that expectations are clear.

Lacrosse games are divided into four quarters or two halves. The length of the game will depend on your organization's rules. Consider using time to determine substitutions. For example, you might tell your team that midway through each quarter, or half, you'll substitute the attackers and defenders. Midfielders will need more frequent breaks, so substitute them every 2 to 3 minutes. Think about how you plan to group the players. Will there be a first team and a second team based on ability, or will you blend your players for team balance? It's your call, but be consistent.

Although you're the coach, and you control playing time in games, you should have established a team philosophy concerning substitution at the preseason meeting with players and parents. Everyone should already be in agreement, so that there are no surprises at the first game.

We recommend that you minimize any methods of substitution that would send a negative message to members of your team, such as not playing some players in "big games," playing some players only when the outcome of the game has been determined, or always starting the same players. To avoid this scenario, try not to place emphasis on players who start the game; instead, focus on the performances of players regardless of when they were on the field. Any effort to place a value on who starts the game might be directed toward behavioral contributions, such as selecting players who attend practice regularly, exhibit the best work habits during practices, or have earned a good listener award. This gives all players an equal opportunity to play first in the game, instead of making athletic ability the sole criterion.

Whatever you, the parents, and the players have selected as team values should be reflected in the way players are sent onto the field during the game. For example, if the team has established a goal that players should improve the quality of their play, then all players should be given equal time during games to develop their talents. Unfortunately, many times the best players on some teams get the most playing time. This means the players who need the most improvement are given the least game time. This occurs most often in an effort to "win" games. The short-term effect of winning the game does not outweigh the long-term process of players' development, however.

Make sure you discuss your substitution plan with your assistant coaches and make one of them responsible for the substituting. This will help you focus on the game and not be distracted by the time it takes to co-ordinate the players.

Make sure that players know that when they substitute they should enter and exit the field through the area by the scorer's table. All players should run on and off the field. Once they're off, they should get a drink and be ready to play again.

Communicating with Players on the Field

One of the most difficult things to do is to communicate with players who are on the field, especially those that are at the opposite end of the field. Assign a leader on each defensive and offensive unit to be the liaison. Choose a player who has a good understanding of the roles of the offense or defense. Communicate with your liaison and then have him communicate with his offensive or defensive teammates on the field. You may want to use large cards to signal a type of defense or offensive play. This way the whole team can see the adjustment, but the liaison should still call it out to teammates. Limit your communication with a player to a particular play. The game moves too fast to analyze every action. Save those discussions for practice when skills can be worked on. Make it very clear to the players that when you communicate with them, it's about lacrosse and how the game is going, not about them personally. If there's a teachable moment when a player comes off the field, have an assistant relay the needed information to the player. This coordination with your coaching staff allows you, the head coach, to focus on the flow of the game, strategy implementation, and the overall play of the team while assistants counsel individual players as needed.

Finally, remind players that parents often get excited at games and that players shouldn't focus on their communications, positive or negative. Make it clear to the parents that their communication should be positive only and that they can discuss plays with their kids after the game on the way home. (See also chapter 7, Dealing with Parents.)

Time-Outs

The time-out is a great rule in lacrosse and can be used in many ways, although learning how to most effectively use time-outs may take some time. Time-outs can be used to stop the momentum of the opposing team, to give your players a rest, to set up a special play on offense or defense, or to get certain players into the game. They can also be used to keep possession if a player is in trouble.

Although rules regarding time-outs may vary from league to league,

Minor Injuries? Think RICE

Bumps and bruises are a part of youth sports. If your player's injury needs more attention than the following, be sure to contact your local emergency room or physician. For minor sprains and strains, however, the RICE method will help a minor soft tissue injury heal faster.

- **Relative Rest.** Avoid activities that exacerbate the injury, but continue to move the injured area gently. Early gentle movement promotes healing.

- **Ice.** Apply ice to the affected area for 20 minutes; then leave it off for at least an hour. Do not use ice if you have circulatory problems.

- **Compression.** Compression creates a pressure gradient that reduces swelling and promotes healing. An elastic bandage provides a moderate amount of pressure that will help discourage swelling.

- **Elevation.** Elevation is especially effective when used in conjunction with compression. Elevation provides a pressure gradient: the higher the injured body part is raised, the more fluid is pulled away from the injury site via gravity. Elevate the injury as high above the heart as comfortable. Continue to elevate intermittently until swelling is gone.

the basic rule is that the team who calls the time-out must have possession of the ball. (Some leagues require you to be in your offensive half of the field.) However, time-outs can be called by either team after a goal, a foul, or when the ball is out-of-bounds.

When you call a time-out, make sure you know why you are doing so. Your players should already know that they need to hustle in and listen because the time-out is limited to 2 minutes. Make your instructions very specific. Explain what you see as a problem and then give a solution. Focus on one aspect of the game only; too many corrections are confusing. If one player is having difficulty with a certain situation, have an assistant talk with him after the team conference. Have the liaisons (or the team or game captains) repeat the problem and solution back to you to make sure they understand, or ask a player who looks confused to explain the problem and solution. Two minutes is plenty of time to make adjustments if you have a plan and if you've used your practices wisely, because it's easy to refer the players to a drill you've used to teach a skill. End the time-out with a team cheer.

Are Statistics Important?

Statistics can be used to motivate players and to determine areas that need work (see the sample on page 130). They can help players focus on a specific skill they want to master or help the team by identifying a fundamental skill that needs improvement. Rewards can be attached to statistics. Helmet stickers can be given for goals scored or assists, for a defensive play, for hustle, for saves, or for ground balls won. Individual recognition is important, but it shouldn't overshadow what the team is trying to accomplish. Develop team rewards for statistics also. If your team scores a goal with an extra-player offense (see pages 46–47) or stops a team during a player-down defensive situation (see page 51), give the offensive or defensive unit a sticker. Make it fun and challenging to earn a reward.

The discussion of statistics should illustrate a teaching point. For example, you might say: "In last weekend's game, we won 20 ground balls. That was 15 fewer than the week before, so we need to work on winning the ground ball this week." Don't get caught in the trap of using statistics to criticize or praise a single player; use them to support team goals. Never use statistics as a way of comparing one player to another: "John, the stats show you won only 2 ground balls in the last game, and Joe won 7." This will detract from the "we" atmosphere you're trying to create.

Questions and Answers

Q. I have a player who doesn't work hard in practice but does very well in games. He says that only games matter. What should I do?

A. It's not uncommon for a player to misunderstand and minimize the importance of practice. Through your planning efforts and by making the practices fun, all players should want to participate. Take another look at your practice plan and make sure that all players are being challenged, that the practices are enjoyable, and that players are learning essential skills. It's quite possible this player has had a bad experience in another sport. Explain the importance of practice as a tool for learning essential skills and team play. Finally, make sure the player is aware of your substitution rules, which may link practice performance to playing time. One player's approach shouldn't compromise your standards and those of the team.

Q. One of my players won't pass the ball during the game. He's fast and moves down the field easily. He shoots most of the time when he gets the ball. Everyone encourages him to pass, but he won't.

A. Begin the solution in practice. Place the player into situations where he has to pass the ball to a variety of players. For example, put a restriction on a drill or scrimmage that each attacker must touch the ball before a shot is taken. Encourage other players to pass to him. It may be that he feels if he passes the ball, no one will pass back it to him. He may have created this problem on his own, but help him solve it by including teammates in the solution. (See drills O1, O4, and O5 on pages 104 and 107–8.)

Q. How should I handle a situation where my team has several dominant players who always want to play together and will only pass to each other when they are in the game?

A. You're not always in control of how quickly players grasp concepts, and you have no control over their size, speed, or coordination. This is where having a good substitution plan will help separate the number of times these players are on the field together. They should have some opportunities to play together, as long as their play is consistent with the expectations of the team. To challenge them, create practice opportunities where players are involved in small-group drill work that occasionally includes only the dominant players.

Q. Our team has some players who are limited in their abilities and have difficulty executing even the most basic fundamentals. How can we get them involved in the game when other players are reluctant to pass to them?

A. Use special situations to get these players involved. Create an extra-player offensive play where they have a key role playing the crease, providing a screen or pick, and converting a *garbage goal* (a goal scored off a rebound or a loose ball in the crease area, not from a direct pass or dodge). Give them the responsibility of backing up the goal on shots. On out-of-bounds plays, have them begin with the ball and set up a *safe first pass* (a relatively short pass to a player in open space). Continue to involve them in small-group drills in practice that offer numerous chances for skill development and decision making. (See drills F4, F6, and F7 on pages 86 and 87–88.)

Q. We found ourselves in a game where things simply weren't going our way. The team was playing poorly, and I began to get frustrated. How can I prevent this from happening?

A. You're not alone. This happens to many coaches, even coaches who have been doing this for a while. You had envisioned something totally different than what was occurring. Keep in mind that even the best plans fall apart. The most important thing to remember is to control the things you can control. Take an aspect of the game and encourage your team to master that in the time remaining. The players will react calmly if you do. Teams are direct reflections of their coaches. If you overreact, so will your team. Take a deep breath and start afresh. Every game and practice is a learning experience, so you'll be better prepared for the next game because of what happened.

Q. We won our first game ever! Several of my players and parents became very excited and began celebrating in a manner that I felt was overexuberant. I was excited, too, but when is a celebration too much?

A. Everyone likes to win. But win or lose, you and your players should display good sportsmanship. Learning to win is sometimes harder than learning to lose. Try to prepare yourself for both outcomes early in the season. Explain to your team how you expect them to act if they win. Tell them that the procedure for winning is the same as for losing: the team gets together immediately following the game to give a cheer for the opposing team, lines up to shake hands with their opponents, and then meets for a brief wrap-up of the game. Players will be more apt to act appropriately if they have been coached in this manner.

Q. Our team played a fantastic game but lost by a large margin. They began to question their abilities and my coaching abilities. How can I refocus them for success?

A. Again, preparation is key. If players know that losing is a possibility, they are more likely to handle it in a positive, sportsmanlike way than if they are never coached on how to handle a loss. Don't coach them on how to lose, but on how to handle a loss—there's a big difference. After the game, follow the same procedures as you do for a win (see previous question). Focus on the things you did well; connect your practice to the successes of the game. You've already established that individual and team success are not based on wins or losses, but on how effectively players performed, a combination of ability, effort, and sportsmanship.

Q. Our team has built a culture around sportsmanship and effort. We make it clear to the players and parents that respecting coaches, teammates, opponents, and officials is paramount. We had a game where the officials were very poor and didn't know the rules of the game. After the game, the players and parents were frustrated by the officials' performance. How should I handle their questions?

A. Lacrosse is a relatively new sport in many areas. Many officials have never played the game or have had only a few opportunities to learn the game. Just as new players learn to build skills and understand the game, officials work to do the same. In many cases, they only get a chance to practice officiating on game day. But players, parents, and coaches should never complain about officials publicly. If your players have questions, talk to them honestly and openly. It sounds like a cliché, but everyone makes mistakes. Sometimes calls will go against your players, and they must learn to accept those calls and move on.

During games, coaches can certainly discuss plays with officials. (The only challenge a coach may make to an official is in a situation where player safety is an issue.) The best way to handle discussions with officials is by asking for clarification, not questioning how the officials saw a play. You should simply offer how you saw the play. The officials may accept your view or stand by how they saw the play. Remember to accept their decision calmly and graciously. Then move on. When handled with respect, most officials are very approachable. They want to do a great job, and most do.

Q. Our team has several players who are very skilled and other players who are just learning the basics of the game. How do I use the same drills at practice for these two different groups?

A. The drills in this book are designed for success for all players, regardless of ability. Developing players can learn in the same setting as advanced players. When you design practices, make sure you group the players so that those with a higher level of ability work with players of lesser ability. This helps to develop leadership in the advanced players as they act as role models. Also, provide some time in practice when players of higher ability are grouped together so they are challenged. Allow the more advanced players to work on a ball drill together to challenge their skills, and group less advanced players together to allow them to develop skills and confidence. When you play with large groups or in gamelike conditions, combine all players and develop the team philosophy. This will eliminate singling out the weaker or better players.

Q. We have players who seem to forget their roles when it comes to game time. How can we change their action during the game?

A. Practice, practice, practice. Set your players up for success. Simulate game conditions during practice. Educate your team on how to set up for face-offs (pages 15 and 39–40), how to *inbound* the ball (one player begins with the ball 5 yards inside the sideline or end line; on the official's whistle, the player may run with the ball or pass it), how to set up for a clear or ride (pages 46 and 51–52), and how to set up for extra-player or player-down play (pages 46–47 and 51). Preparation is again a key factor. In addition, put assistant coaches in charge of certain players. When the player comes out of the game, the assistant can talk to them about their role.

CHAPTER 7

Dealing with Parents

One of the best pieces of advice we can give coaches is to realize that "parents are people, too." They have needs, wants, and emotions. Their feelings are typically guided by the desire to have their children excel. Aren't we lucky as coaches? That's exactly what we want too! You may be surprised at how quickly your parents become positive and develop a sense of trust when you let them know at your preseason meeting that you share that common ground with them. Once again, communication is the key.

Ask parents at the preseason meeting what they want from this lacrosse experience for their child. As described in chapter 1 (see pages 6–7), make a list of goals and objectives to be accomplished by the end of the season. Continue to reinforce these goals and objectives during practices, games, team dinners, parent newsletters, casual conversations, and team meetings. Communicate, communicate, communicate. This will open up a dialogue between you and the parents and will be the catalyst for your helping them see the big picture. If you start out knowing what you want to accomplish by the end of the season—with the goals and objectives for the team established by the parents, players, and coaches—then every practice plan, game, coaching decision, and parent comment should lead to the end product. This helps give direction and focus to everyone's efforts and helps minimize behavior that doesn't help lead the team members toward achieving their goals and objectives.

This process helps eliminate confusion by the parties involved. And because you included the parents and players in the decision-making process concerning goals and objectives for the season, they're more likely to be positive because they have a sense of ownership in the process. It's simple. They know what the goals are because they helped to create them. Helping to achieve the goals motivates every action.

A critical part of this interaction process with the parents is letting them know that you need their assistance in meeting the goals and objectives agreed upon while reinforcing that you're the coach. Clearly outline for them how they can help with such things as field maintenance, uniform distribution, fund-raising, or any of the other responsibilities that you've taken on. Make your authority as coach understood in a gracious manner, but try to involve parents as much as possible. This will help prevent parents from criticizing players, officials, strategy, or other aspects of your coaching.

At the preseason meeting, explain that it's your role to critique players and that you'll do so in a positive manner while meeting people on a courteous level of mutual self-respect. The preseason meeting is the parent's first chance to see how organized you are. Parents appreciate this because lack of organization breeds confusion. Show parents your organizational skills by having written plans for practice and games, by being punctual, and by being regular in attendance. Communication through parent letters and follow-up phone calls also is a good sign of being organized. And when you communicate with the parents, always maintain your emotional control. Have a sense of humor. Humor goes a long way in disarming people. Let them know it's OK to disagree, but remind them that the way they display their disagreement should be respectful.

Some of the toughest situations for coaches occur when people associated with the team place too much emphasis on winning games (see the sidebar on page 8). You'll do yourself, your players, and their parents a huge favor by helping them redefine winning at your preseason meeting. Many people (players, parents, and, sadly, some coaches) regard winning the game as being successful and losing the game as being unsuccessful.

This places too much pressure on the need to win the game because no one wants to be unsuccessful. It sometimes leads to a "do or die" attitude and the loss of emotional control. Instead, the coach should help guide the thinking of those involved with the team so they understand that being successful can be measured by accomplishing the goals and objectives that were developed, improving skills and concepts, and having the courage to participate.

Remember that your task as a youth coach is a big one. You're going to need all the support you can muster. Get parents involved in a positive way so that everyone's working to benefit the children. The greater the effort you make to this commitment, the easier your job will become.

Questions and Answers

Q. I have some parents who want their sons, who are quite good players, to play more during games. I have explained that it's important for all team members to have game experience, regardless of ability, but they won't accept this. How do I handle this?

A. At your preseason meeting with parents and players, you should take

Sample Preseason Letter to Parents

Dear Parents:

Another lacrosse season is upon us. I'm excited about our team and hope your kids are, too.

My primary goal for the season is for everyone to have fun and improve their lacrosse skills. My basic philosophy is to foster a positive, supportive atmosphere so that every player has a great experience. Regardless of ability, every member of the team deserves to be treated with encouragement. Players should respect each other on and off the field and should learn both to win and lose well. I look to you to help reinforce these important concepts: when you come to games or practices, please limit your interaction with your children to positive encouragement from a distance. During games, please treat the officials with the respect they deserve. We are our children's most important role models. I'll set as good an example as I possibly can, and I would greatly appreciate your help by doing the same.

Games: Please make every effort to arrive at games 30 minutes before the scheduled start. If you know that getting your child to a game will be difficult, we can carpool. If your child can't make it to a game, please let me know in advance. If he misses practice the week before the game without a good reason, he might not play in the game. Please know that I have this policy so that participation in the games is fair to everyone.

Cancellation: Unless you hear otherwise, we'll always have practice or games. In the case of cancellation, kids will be notified either at school or by means of the enclosed phone tree.

Must bring: Please make sure that your child has a water bottle, gloves, and appropriate shoes. These, and other personal equipment (arm and shoulder pads, helmet, stick) should be labeled with his name.

We're looking forward to a great season of lacrosse. If you have any questions or concerns, please feel free to contact me.

Thanks,
The Coach
204 Maple Avenue
555-1234
coach@lacrosse.com

Calling All Volunteers!

If you have parents who want to be part of the team but don't want to help out on the field, by all means use their enthusiasm to take over the administrative details. There are routine but important administrative aspects to running a team that could be taken over by a manager or several committed parents:

Phone Tree

Instead of having every kid call you whenever there's a threat of a shower or a change in the schedule, have one parent arrange a phone tree. You can call one designated person, who then initiates a reliable chain of communication for the rest of the team.

Practice Transportation

A designated parent can be in charge of carpooling by checking that each player has a ride to practice and home again. Though many families won't need this help, the safety net it provides for those who do is re-assuring. This parent should make certain that all players are picked up from practice before he or she leaves.

Away-Game Transportation

It's a great idea to have a centrally located place where kids can meet before going to away games. A designated parent can schedule the time and place for meeting before away games and can make sure that there will be enough drivers to accommodate the players and that drivers have written directions to the field. Meeting like this before the game ensures that each player is accounted for and has a ride to the game, and it also builds team unity before the game.

Fund-Raisers

Getting all of the necessary equipment can be somewhat expensive. Having team dinners, organizing fund drives, and arranging other fund-raising events are projects that an administrative parent can orga-nize, with some of the duties delegated to other team parents as well.

Snack Duties

A small, nutritious snack during practice or a trip to the ice cream stand after a game can be a helpful boost or well-deserved reward for your young players. A parent can be in charge of this service or can cre-ate a rotating schedule of parents who would be interested in helping. This is a fun and highly satisfying way that parents can become involved with the team.

the time to explain the team's philosophy about playing time during games. Most likely, the kids will agree to equal playing time. Make it clear then that, no matter the game situation, you'll be scheduling equal playing time for each player. Youth players will develop at differ-ent rates; some will have rapid success while others will take more time. But all players need game minutes.

It's likely that those parents who want their kids to have more game time are more interested in winning than in player develop-ment. Now is probably a good time to remind them of the pre-season meeting when you, the players, and the parents agreed to the team goals (see page 7). Remind the parents that the team defines "success" as player and team development, not winning individual games.

Q. I have a parent who wants his son to play only positions where he can score goals. He pays his son $1 for each goal he scores during games. What's a diplomatic solution here?

A. We've had the same problem. Some parents think it motivates players to offer money for goals scored. This often leads to selfish play that works against the team's goals. But lots of attention is given to players who score goals, and regrettably, that's what some parents and players become focused on.

     We suggest making it clear to players and parents that everyone contributes to scoring goals. Don't emphasize who scored the goal, but focus on the movement, communication, and skills that led to the final act of shooting a goal. Thus, don't have leading scorer awards, or announce the weekly statistics of who has scored the most goals. Instead, praise things like the great goalie clear that started the scoring opportunity, or the great defensive play that gave your team possession of the ball.

     If you choose to use goal-scoring statistics, then we suggest that you also use statistics for other valued elements of the game, such as scooping ground balls, deflecting passes by opponents, player communication, etc. This values the participation and contributions of all the players.

Q. During our preseason meeting, we discussed our commitment to good sportsmanship, but the players (and some of the parents) are having a hard time honoring it during games, especially when we're losing. How can I get them back on track?

A. There's no getting around it: losing is hard. But remember to keep your players and the parents focused on the team goals you discussed at the preseason meeting and the goals you've discussed during practices and before each game. Emphasize what the team did well, and have players come up with a list of skills the team should work on at the next practice.

     One way to help is by having a "sportsmanship assessment meeting" after each game with players and parents. From the preseason meeting, develop an evaluation form for players that includes things like "accepts authority of officials," "plays within the rules of the game," "respects opponents," etc. Items for parents might include "treats other parents with respect," "comments positively about player performance," and "respects officials." And don't forget a section for coaches! Have ratings like "great," "needs improvement," and "OK." Tabulate the results right there and discuss them with the group. Don't single out individuals, but make your comments general and as positive as possible: "Wow, you guys worked really well with the officials today, but remember it's important to graciously shake hands with our opponents after the game." Or, "I apologize for getting frustrated during the second half. You guys played really hard today, and I'm proud of your effort and team spirit." Or, "Let's give a big thank you to all the parents who came out and cheered for us today! Those encouraging words really help." By involving everyone in the process, you'll make everyone accountable for their actions during games and make good sportsmanship a goal for everyone aspire to.

Fundamental Drills

Every player needs to work on fundamentals. The drills in this chapter provide the basis for being successful in gamelike situations and in games. Take the opportunity to teach and make corrections as the players work. These drills are designed for repetition and a great deal of movement. They are conducted using stations, and there should be several drills occurring at the same time. No players should be standing around waiting for their turn. The tempo of these fundamental drills should be as fast-paced as is appropriate for the skill level of your players: fast enough to challenge your players while encouraging learning and success.

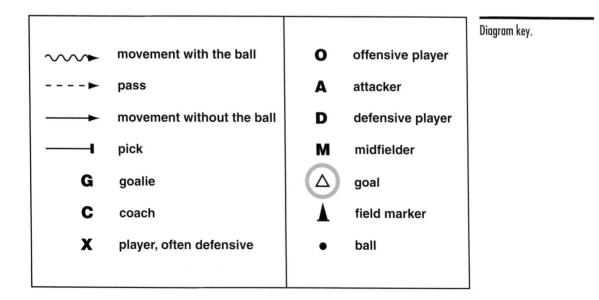

~~►	movement with the ball		O	offensive player
– – –►	pass		A	attacker
──►	movement without the ball		D	defensive player
──┤	pick		M	midfielder
G	goalie		△	goal
C	coach		▲	field marker
X	player, often defensive		●	ball

Diagram key.

Warm-Up Drills

Grid Tag F1

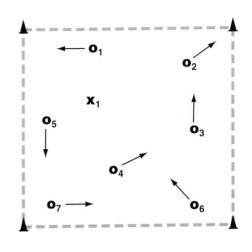

Purpose:
To learn the fundamentals of space and movement and to build agility and quickness.

Number of Players:
8 (1 defensive player, 7 offensive players)

Equipment:
4 field markers, 1–4 practice jerseys

1. Establish a 30-by-30-yard grid. **2.** Players should space themselves evenly around the grid. **3.** The defensive player X1 holding a jersey attempts to tag any offensive player in the grid. **4.** The defender begins with a 5-second countdown. **5.** The offensive players must move around inside the grid and try to avoid being tagged. **6.** If caught, the offensive player takes the jersey and becomes the defender. **7.** The new defender can't catch the original defender but must attempt to get other players. **8.** Modify by adding defenders one at a time. **9.** Players should wear full equipment and hold their sticks in two hands.

The game of tag is basic to the concept of understanding open and closed space. An offensive player needs to move to *open space*, an area without defenders or other offensive players, by scanning and making good decisions about where to move and how to get there without coming in contact with others. Helping players understand space and movement and giving them the opportunity to make decisions will make teaching the game of lacrosse considerably easier.

Missing Marker F2

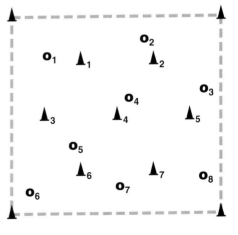

Purpose:
To change speed and direction.

Number of Players:
8

Equipment:
11 field markers

1. Create a 20-by-20-yard grid with four of the field markers. **2.** Place the remaining seven markers inside the grid, spacing them appropriately. **3.** Space the eight players in the grid. **4.** Players begin on your signal. **5.** Players move through the grid until the whistle. **6.** On the whistle, players must move to a marker and remain there until you begin play again. **7.** One player won't be able to find an unclaimed marker. **8.** This player is eliminated from the round. He must go outside the grid, where he picks up a stick and works on cradling the ball with both hands and with one hand. **9.** A marker is removed, and players begin. **10.** When the next player is eliminated, the first player returns. **11.** The drill continues for 2 minutes, with each player trying not to be eliminated.

Coaches shouldn't use games where players are eliminated for long periods of time. You need to design elimination games so that eliminated players are allowed to return to the action after a brief period of time. To encourage fast-paced movement, insist that players move around and touch at least four markers before the whistle blows.

Changing Partners F3

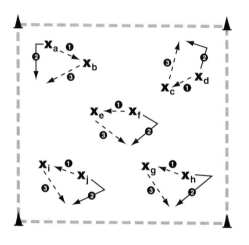

1. Create a 20-by-20-yard grid. **2.** Space the partners around the grid in open space. **3.** Play begins with one player (player Xa in the first group) passing to his stationary partner (player Xb in the first group). **4.** The first player then makes a cut to receive a return pass. When he catches the return pass, he must find another stationary player to pass to. The other pairs of players are doing the same. There will be five stationary and five moving players. **5.** Play continues for several minutes to allow players lots of touches on the ball. **6.** Players switch roles, and the drill continues.

Purpose:
To improve vision, communication, and decision making with the ball.
Number of Players:
10 (5 groups of 2)
Equipment:
4 field markers, 5 balls

As players move through the grid, they should remain aware of the other players. This is accomplished by scanning the grid to find the open spaces and stationary players. Players should move purposefully, working hard to maintain grid balance (even spacing). The drill is very good for promoting communication.

FUNDAMENTAL DRILLS

Inside-Out F4

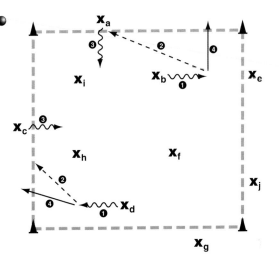

Purpose:
To develop good
habits of vision,
communication,
and movement.
Number of Players:
10
Equipment:
4 field markers,
5 balls

1. Create a 20-by-20-yard grid.
2. Five players begin inside
the grid with a ball. **3.** Five
players begin outside the grid
without a ball. **4.** Play begins
with the players inside the
grid moving with the ball toward a player outside the grid.
5. Each player inside the grid
passes to a player outside the
grid and then moves outside
the grid. **6.** Each player outside the grid moves into the
grid with the ball and must pass to a player outside the grid other than the
player who passed to him. **7.** Play is continuous.

Initially this drill looks very simple. As the ball is dropped or the players begin to move in different direc-
tions and at different speeds, it
becomes important for players to
communicate effectively. Players
discover that players and space
become closed quickly.

Passing and Catching Drills

Catch and Turn Away F5

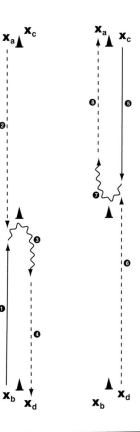

Purpose:
To catch and
change direction.
Number of Players:
4
Equipment:
3 field markers,
1 ball

1. Create a line of three field markers with 10 yards between each
marker. **2.** Two players stand behind
each outside field marker. **3.** The
ball begins with player Xa (see left
illustration). **4.** Player Xb cuts toward player Xa. **5.** Player Xa passes
to player Xb. Player Xa returns to
the marker and goes behind player
Xc. **6.** Player Xb catches the ball

and turns back toward the marker where he started. **7.** Player Xb passes to player Xd. **8.** Player Xc cuts toward the center marker and receives the pass from player Xd (see right illustration). **9.** Player Xc turns and passes to player Xa. Player Xc goes behind player Xa in line. **10.** Player Xa catches and passes to player Xd who is cutting toward the center marker. **11.** Play is continuous.

This simple passing and catching drill allows players lots of repetitions and teaches technique and the basic movements of cutting to the pass, catching, and changing direction. The drill should be completed left- and right-handed.

Triangle F6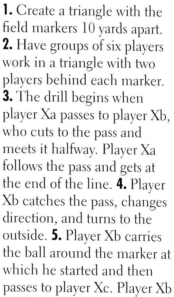

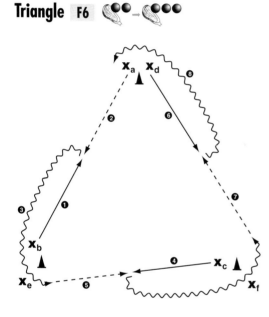

1. Create a triangle with the field markers 10 yards apart. **2.** Have groups of six players work in a triangle with two players behind each marker. **3.** The drill begins when player Xa passes to player Xb, who cuts to the pass and meets it halfway. Player Xa follows the pass and gets at the end of the line. **4.** Player Xb catches the pass, changes direction, and turns to the outside. **5.** Player Xb carries the ball around the marker at which he started and then passes to player Xc. Player Xb follows his pass and gets in the back of the line. **6.** Player Xc moves to meet the pass, turns outside, carries around the marker, and passes to player Xd. Player Xc follows his pass and gets in the back of the line. **7.** Player Xd moves to meet the pass, turns outside, carries around the marker, and passes to player Xe. Player Xd follows his pass and gets in the back of the line. **8.** Play continues.

Purpose:
To teach the fundamentals of passing and catching.

Number of Players:
6

Equipment:
3 field markers, 2 balls

It's important for the players to catch the pass with the stick to the outside of the triangle. This keeps the stick away from defensive pressure in game situations. The turn to the outside simulates a change of direction. The carrying of the ball around the marker makes the passer feed while on the run, an essential of feeding.

Four-Corner Hot Potato   F7

Purpose:
To move the ball quickly and to move without the ball.

Number of Players:
4

Equipment:
4 field markers, 1 ball

1. Create a 15-by-15-yard grid.
2. One defensive player takes the middle. **3.** The three offensive players take positions on the outside by the markers. **4.** Players O1, O2, and O3 work to play catch around the perimeter of the grid.
5. The defender (D1) pressures the pass and tries to intercept.
6. Player O1 begins with the ball and has player O2 to his left and player O3 to his right, providing two adjacent passing options.
7. Player O1 can pass to player O2 or O3. **8.** If player O1 passes to player O2, player O3 must move to the open adjacent marker.
9. If player O1 passes to player O3, player O2 must move to the open adjacent marker. **10.** Players continue to pass and move for several minutes; switch the defender in the middle and start again.

Players begin to understand that it's important to move without the ball. When a player remains stationary, this limits the ability of the offensive players to get a pass to him. The drill also allows the offensive players to see how passing lanes can be lost without movement and with the presence of the defender's stick in the passing lane.

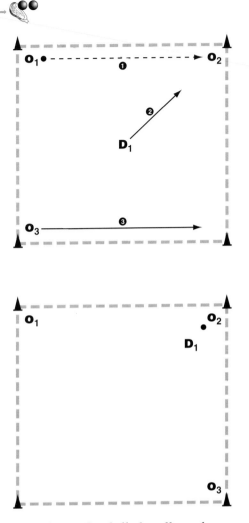

Diamond Transition F8

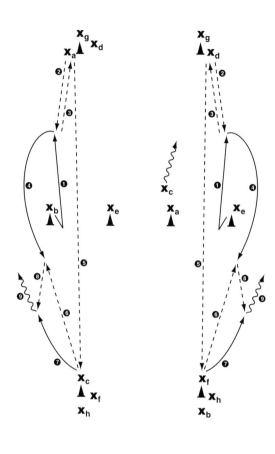

1. Create a 30-by-20-yard diamond shape. **2.** Players take the positions as shown (see left illustration). **3.** Player Xa begins by passing to player Xb. **4.** Player Xb cuts to the ball, catches it, and passes back to player Xa. **5.** Player Xb then turns outside and cuts around the marker toward player Xc. **6.** Player Xa passes to player Xc. **7.** Player Xc catches the ball and executes a *give-and-go* with player Xb, where player Xb receives the pass from player Xc and then passes it back to player Xc. In a game situation, a give-and-go involves "going" past the defender. **8.** Player Xc then carries the ball around the marker and replaces player Xa. **9.** Player Xa replaces player Xb, and player Xb replaces player Xc. **10.** On the second pass by player Xa (step 6),

Purpose:
To learn off-the-ball movement and how to create passing lanes.
Number of Players:
8
Equipment:
4 field markers, 4 balls

player Xd starts a ball on the other side of the diamond by passing to player Xe (see right illustration). **11.** Player Xe cuts to the ball, catches it, and passes back to player Xd. **12.** Player Xe turns outside and cuts around the marker toward player Xf. **13.** Player Xd passes to player Xf. **14.** Player Xf catches the ball and executes a give-and-go with player Xe. **15.** Player Xf then carries the ball around the drill and replaces player Xd. **16.** Player Xd replaces player Xe, and player Xe replaces player Xf. Continue with players Xg and Xh. **17.** Play is continuous.

This drill involves many basic concepts of passing and catching. It gives the players a chance to work on techniques by having lots of repetitions. The drill also effectively combines concepts of movement and passing. The give-and-go is executed twice. Players are encouraged to move without the ball and to work on the timing of their runs.

Team Diagonals F9

Purpose:
To cut on diagonals, creating space and opening up passing lanes.

Number of Players:
10

Equipment:
4 field markers, 10 balls

1. Create four diagonally offset lines spaced 30 yards apart and covering a length of approximately 70 yards. **2.** Place a goalie about 20 yards from each end. **3.** Goalie G1 has all the balls and begins the drill. **4.** Player G1 calls "clear" or "break," and player O1 cuts diagonally across the field toward player O2. **5.** Player O1 catches the ball and immediately looks to pass to diagonally cutting player O2. **6.** Player O2 catches the and immediately looks to pass to diagonally cutting player O3. **7.** On this pass, goalie G1 begins a second ball by passing to player O5. **8.** Play continues with player O3 passing to player O4, who cuts diagonally. **9.** Player O4 passes to goalie G2. **10.** All players return to the line where they began. **11.** Play continues until all balls are with goalie G2. **12.** G2 starts the drill in the other direction.

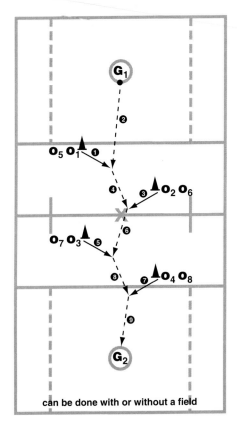

can be done with or without a field

The timing of the diagonal run is important. The receiving player should have full vision of the pass in front of him and shouldn't have to catch over his shoulder. It's also important that players develop the ability to pass and catch on the run.

Scooping Drills

Grid Keep-Away F10

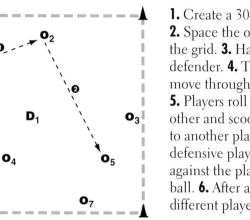

1. Create a 30-by-30-yard grid. 2. Space the offensive players in the grid. 3. Have one player be a defender. 4. The offensive players move throughout the grid. 5. Players roll the ball to each other and scoop the ball and roll to another player while the one defensive player tries to defend against the player scooping the ball. 6. After a few minutes have a different player be the defender.

Purpose:
To practice scooping with defensive pressure and limited space.
Number of Players:
8
Equipment:
4 field markers,
1 practice jersey,
3 balls

The role of the defender in this drill is to place enough pressure on an offensive player to force him to make decisions related to vision, rather than to try to take the ball away or intercept a ground ball. Be sure the defender is moving toward the ground ball. The offensive players should scoop, tuck, and change directions. The *tuck* is the motion of bringing the ball to the box area. The ball should then be rolled to a player who is in open space. Modify the drill by adding a defender, adding a ball, or both.

One-on-One Ground Balls F11

1. Create three lines 5 yards apart. 2. Two players stand behind each line (see top illustration next page). 3. You start the drill by standing behind the lines and rolling a ball 10 yards in front of the line. 4. On your whistle or signal, the players run to scoop the ground ball. 5. Each player is working alone to get the ball. 6. Once a player has scooped the ball, he passes it to one of the other players. The third player becomes a defender. 7. The play continues back to you as a two-on-one. 8. Play ends with a successful pass to you (see bottom illustration).

Purpose:
To develop the fundamentals of scooping a ground ball under pressure.
Number of Players:
6
Equipment:
3 field markers,
2 balls

Players should attack the ground ball with speed, with each player trying to use his body to get between the ball and the other players. Once the scoop has occurred, emphasize movement without the ball and communication to receive a pass. The drill is great for teaching the importance of the ground ball. A traditional variation has the two outside lines competing against the inside line. Here one outside player takes the ball, and the other

FUNDAMENTAL DRILLS

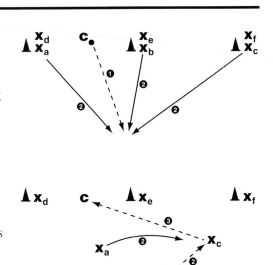

outside player works to shield the inside player from the ball with a body check. The two players communicate by calling out *man* (identifies the outside player who shields the inside player from the ball) and *ball* (identifies the outside player who takes the ball). Once a player has scooped the ball, he should communicate "ball" to signal he has possession, and his partner needs to move to open space to receive a pass.

Alternate Triangle F12

Purpose:
To learn proper techniques of scooping and finishing the scoop.

Number of Players:
6

Equipment:
3 field markers, 2 balls

1. Create a triangle with the markers 10 yards apart. **2.** Two players stand behind each marker. **3.** Play begins with player Xa rolling to player Xb. **4.** Player Xb begins his move with a V-cut and moves toward the ball, scoops it, and then turns to the outside of the triangle. **5.** He carries the ball around his marker and passes to player Xc. **6.** Player Xc begins with a V-cut and moves toward the ball; he catches it and then turns to the outside of the triangle. **7.** Player Xc carries the ball around the marker and rolls it to player Xd. **8.** Play continues with alternate passing and rolling of the ball.

The idea of alternating the scooping and passing is important because it forces players to bring the stick into the box area, complete the scoop with a tuck, and change direction. Players will get lazy sticks if they're allowed to simply roll the ball to the next player. All players should return to the line where they started.

Half-Field Team Scramble F13

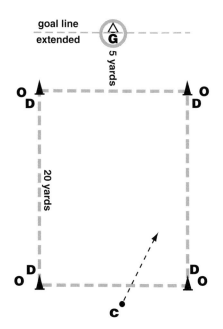

1. Create a grid 5 yards above the *goal line extended* (an imaginary extension of the goal line), with a goal centered at one end and the markers 20 yards apart. **2.** Place an offensive player and a defensive player at each marker. All eight are involved in the play, and the goalie is in the goal. **3.** Play begins with a ground ball from you toward one of the four markers. **4.** The players at the marker battle for the ball. **5.** If the offensive team wins the ground ball, play continues until a shot, goal, steal, or save occurs. **6.** If the defensive team wins the ground ball, play continues until the defense can pass to the goalie and clear the ball back to you.

Purpose:
To emphasize the importance of the ground ball to team success.
Number of Players:
9 (1 goalie, 4 offensive players, 4 defenders)
Equipment:
4 field markers, 5 balls, 4 practice jerseys

Anticipation of the ground ball is essential. It's also important for a player to get to the ball as quickly as possible to win the scoop outright or to use his body to shield the other player. All players are encouraged to scoop, tuck, and change direction away from the pressure of the opponent. Younger players tend to turn back into the defensive pressure (turn toward their opponent), but this can be reduced by having the players peek over their shoulder and scan as they're moving with speed to the ball. Once the scoop is completed, vision becomes important because it allows players to get the information they need to decide whether to pass, dodge, shoot, or maintain possession.

The Gauntlet F14

1. Organize the players as shown (see illustration next page). There should be about 10 yards between players Xa and Xb and players Xc and Xd, and about 15 yards between players Xc and Xd and player Xe. **2.** The ball is between players Xc and Xd, who are standing 5 feet apart, with their sticks forming an X in front of the ball. **3.** Player Xa runs and scoops the ball through the sticks of players Xc and Xd. **4.** Player Xa finishes the scoop with a tuck, change of direction, and pass to player Xe. **5.** Player Xe has cut on a diagonal in the opposite direction from player Xa's change of direction. **6.** Player Xe passes to player Xd, replaces player Xc, joins player Xd with crossed sticks, and waits for the next player to scoop the ball through the sticks. **7.** Player Xa replaces

Purpose:
To scoop under stick pressure and finish with a pass.
Number of Players:
5
Equipment:
2 balls

player Xe, player Xc goes behind player Xb, and player Xb continues the drill with a scoop. **8.** Play is continuous, with each player getting ten to fifteen repetitions.

The scooping player needs to scoop through the sticks. This simulates the pressure of a stick check during a game. It's important for the player to lower his body properly and allow the upper arms and shoulders to assist taking the crossed sticks out of play. The player should tuck and gain vision quickly so that the pass can be executed.

Dodging Drills

Grid Explosion F15

Purpose:
To learn the fundamental technique of dodging.
Number of Players:
10
Equipment:
4 field markers, 5 balls

1. Create a 20-by-20-yard grid. **2.** Space five players evenly throughout the grid. These players are the dodging obstacles. **3.** Space the remaining five players in the grid, each with a ball. **4.** Play begins on your command or whistle. **5.** The player with the ball attacks a stationary player and executes a dodge. **6.** The player with the ball changes direction and dodges another stationary player. **7.** Play continues for 2 minutes, and then the players switch roles.

Dodging is a technique used to create space when under defensive pressure. Dodging involves feinting in one direction in an attempt to have the opponent shift his position and then quickly changing direction to an open space. There are several types of dodges that may be used, including the roll dodge, face dodge, and split dodge (see pages 33–36). Players should approach a stationary player with as much speed as possible, making sure the dodge is executed correctly. Once the dodge is completed, the player should explode out of the dodge to gain space quickly. Focus on footwork, body balance, and stick position during the dodge. Players should execute a different dodge each time they approach a stationary player. Modify the defensive role and allow the defender to give one check and take one backward, or drop, step. This promotes better defensive position and requires the offense to execute a proper dodge.

Pass and Dodge F16

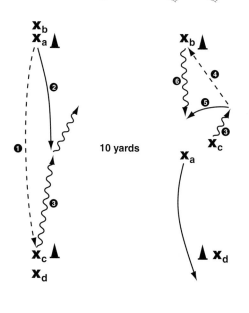

1. Place two field markers 10 yards apart. 2. Two players are behind each marker (see left illustration). 3. Play begins with player Xa. 4. Xa passes to player Xc and follows his pass to the middle of the markers. 5. Player Xc catches the ball and attacks the middle of the markers and player Xa. 6. Player Xc executes a dodge on player Xa. 7. Player Xc passes to player Xb, player Xa replaces player Xc, and play continues with player Xb dodging player Xc (see right illustration). 8. Player Xb passes to player Xd, and player Xd dodges player Xb. 9. Play is continuous.

Purpose:
To develop dodging technique under moderate pressure.
Number of Players:
4
Equipment:
2 field markers, 1 ball

Players will need to read the center player to determine what type of dodge to execute. For example, if the defender has his stick straight out as if to poke check, the player should execute a roll dodge. If the defender's stick is up, the player should execute a face dodge or split dodge (see pages 35–36). Center players should vary their stick positions to encourage a variety of dodges. This drill forces players to complete the dodge and exit ready to feed, with their heads up for vision.

Gauntlet Take a Check F17

Purpose:
To take a slap check and continue the attack.

Number of Players:
6 (2 defenders, 4 attackers)

Equipment:
2 field markers, 2 balls

1. Place two markers 30 yards apart. **2.** Two players stand behind each marker. The two remaining players stand between the two markers about 10 yards from each other. **3.** Player A1 begins. **4.** Player A1 attacks toward the opposite line. **5.** Player A1 approaches player D1 and takes a slap check from D1. **6.** Player A1 continues toward player D2 and executes a dodge. **7.** Player A1 completes the dodge by passing to player A3. **8.** Player A1 goes to the back of the line. **9.** Player A3 attacks toward the opposite line, taking a slap check from player D2 and dodging player D1. **10.** Player A3 passes to player A2, and play continues. **11.** After five runs, switch defenders.

Many times players will begin attacking toward the goal because they have open space. When defenders recover to close the space, they lead with their sticks, and many times this is the only way they can make contact with the attacking player. Attackers need to learn to run through this desperation check in order to keep the attacking move alive. The slap by player D1 should be a light check to the stick. Player D2 should play passively at first and progress to moderate and gamelike defensive pressure.

Small-Grid Dodging F18

Purpose:
To develop dodging techniques while in limited space.

Number of Players:
2

Equipment:
4 field markers, 1 ball

1. Create a 10-by-10-yard grid. **2.** Place two players in the grid, one a defender and one an offensive player. **3.** Player D1 begins with the ball and passes to player O1. **4.** Player O1's objective is to dodge past player D1 and cross the imaginary line between the two markers on the defensive side of the grid. **5.** Play continues until player D1 steals the ball, player O1 scores by making it over the line, or player O1 is forced outside the grid (out-of-bounds). **6.** The game continues until one player reaches 5 points. One point is given to player O1 if he makes it across the line, and 1 point is given to player D1 if he steals the ball or forces player O1 outside the grid.

The offensive player needs to attack the defensive player and cause him to move side to side or to lose his proper defensive stance. When this occurs, the offensive player has the advantage. The limited space helps the attacking player keep a narrow line to goal in a gamelike situation. With better stick-handling players, you may want to reduce the grid to 6 yards or less on each side.

Attack Dodge to Goal F19

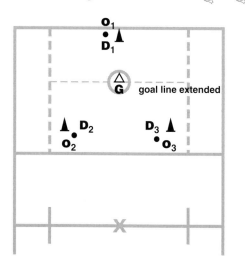

1. Place the field markers as shown in the diagram, one at a point behind the end line, one about 10 yards above the goal line extended left, and one 10 yards above the goal line extended right. **2.** One defender and one offensive player position themselves by each marker. **3.** Play begins by the goalie calling for the players at the right, left, or end line position to attack the goal. **4.** The offensive player works to score from the position called out. This player has 5 seconds, because the drill has gamelike pressure. **5.** Play continues from each marker, one marker at a time. **6.** After three rotations, offensive players should switch markers.

Purpose:
To develop tactical awareness of how to use proper lines and angle to attack the goal.

Number of Players:
7 (1 goalie, 3 offensive players, 3 defenders)

Equipment:
1 goal, 3 field markers, 3 balls

This drill can be played as a game, giving the offensive player one point for a shot and two for a goal, and one point to the defense for a steal or stop. Emphasize a direct line to the goal and a change of speed and direction to set up the dodge.

FUNDAMENTAL DRILLS

Midfield Dodging to Goal F20

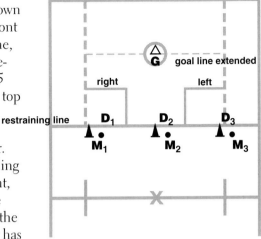

Purpose:
To develop tactical awareness of how to use proper lines and angles to attack the goal.

Number of Players:
7 (1 goalie, 3 defenders, 3 midfielders)

Equipment:
1 goal, 3 field markers, 1 ball

1. Place the field markers as shown in the diagram, one at center front 5 yards above the restraining line, one about 5 yards outside the restraining line top left, and one 5 yards above the restraining line top right. **2.** One defender and one midfielder should position themselves by each marker. **3.** Play begins by the goalie calling for the player at the center, right, or left to attack the goal. **4.** The midfielder works to score from the position called out. This player has 5 seconds, because the drill has gamelike conditions. **5.** Play continues from each marker, one marker at a time. **6.** After three rotations, midfielders players should switch markers.

This drill can be played as a game, giving midfielders one point for a shot and two for a goal, and one point to the defense for a steal or stop. Emphasize a direct line to the goal and a change of speed and direction to set up the dodge.

Shooting Drills

Rapid Fire F21

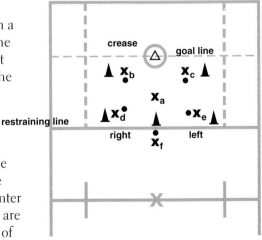

Purpose:
To develop the technique of catching and releasing a quick shot.

Number of Players:
6

Equipment:
1 goal, 5 field markers, 5 balls

1. Field markers are arranged in a five-pointed star pattern, with the bottom point at center front just inside the restraining line. **2.** The other four markers are located at top left and at top right, just inside the restraining line, and at low left and at low right, 5 yards above the goal line extended and 10 yards from the crease. **3.** Player X_a is in the center of the star. **4.** The other players are feeders and are located at each of the markers. Each player has a ball. **5.** Play begins when player Xa calls to one of the other players for a pass. **6.** Player Xa catches the ball and shoots on goal. **7.** Player Xa continues until he's received a pass from all players. **8.** Then a new player takes the center spot, and play continues.

The shooter should be in motion and try to receive passes on diagonal cuts. This allows him to keep the goal in sight. If a player has to catch a pass with his back to the goal, he should continue his feet in motion as he receives the pass and then square to the goal while moving. A player who stops will have difficulty shooting in gamelike situations. The shooter should cut with two hands on the stick and with the head of the stick in the box area. He should avoid extending his arms too far to catch the pass. This action will invite a defender to throw a slap check across the forearms of the shooter during gamelike situations. This drill can be modified to add a defender on the shooter or feeders and by adding a goalie.

Crease Attack   F22

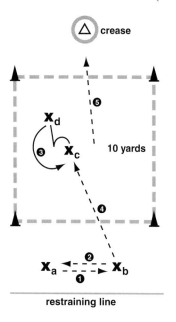

1. Create a 10-by-10-yard grid centered on the goal 5 yards above the crease. **2.** Two players, Xa and Xb, serve as feeders and begin about 5 yards inside the restraining line. Two other players, Xc and Xd, take positions inside the crease grid. **3.** Players Xa and Xb pass the ball back and forth, looking to feed to attackers Xc and Xd in the grid. **4.** Players Xc and Xd must execute a pick in order to receive the pass. **5.** The pass comes from player Xa to player Xc or Xd, whoever is coming off the pick. The player in the grid who didn't get the pass follows to the goal for a rebound. **6.** Play continues with players Xa and Xb passing to one another and waiting to pass to a crease grid player coming off a pick.

Purpose:
To develop the tactical use of the pick to create space for receiving a pass and shooting.
Number of Players:
4
Equipment:
1 goal, 4 field markers, 5 balls

During the drill, the crease grid players Xc and Xd should be at different levels—that is, different distances from the goal. Players should also be opposite each other. For example, if one player is in the low right of the grid, the other player should be in the top left. The crease players keep their eyes on the top players and wait for them to be ready to feed before setting a pick. Once they realize the top player is a feeder, one player picks for the other. If the feed doesn't come, the grid players work to different levels and begin again. This drill can be modified by adding a defender to the grid and by adding a goalie. The same drill can be run from behind with the midfielder in the grid and the attackers passing behind the goal and then moving to enter the feeding area. To get the player setting the pick involved and to stress the importance of following shots to get rebounds and garbage goals, you can roll a ball out to the second pick player after a shot and when the second pick player rushes in to get the rebound. He picks up the ball and shoots it into the goal for the garbage goal.

Shooting Gallery F23

Purpose:
To develop the give-and-go tactic and finish with a shot.
Number of Players:
8 (4 attackers, 4 midfielders)
Equipment:
1 goal, 4 field markers, 10 balls

1. Create a grid with the goal centered at one end. Place one marker low left about 10 yards wide of the goal and 5 yards above the crease, another marker low right about 10 yards wide of the goal and 5 yards above the crease, another marker 10 yards wide of the goal and 5 yards inside the restraining line and to the left, and the remaining marker 10 yards wide of the goal and 5 yards inside the restraining line at top right. **2.** The drill begins with the attacking players in possession of the ball. **3.** Attacker A1 passes to midfielder M1. **4.** Attacker A1 then cuts to the goal, and midfielder M1 passes back to attacker A1, completing the give-and-go. **5.** A1 finishes with a shot. **6.** The same steps are completed by attacker A2 and midfielder M2, attacker A3 and midfielder M3, and attacker A4 and midfielder M4. **7.** Play is continuous. Attackers shoot for three rounds and then switch roles with the midfielders. **8.** The drill begins again with midfielder M1 passing to attacker A1. **9.** Midfielder M1 cuts to goal, and attacker A1 passes to midfielder M1. **10.** M1 finishes with a shot on goal. **11.** The same steps are completed by players A2 and M2, A3 and M3, and A4 and M4.

All passes or feeds should be done with the player in motion. The player should receive the pass on the run and take a shot on the run. Encourage attackers to *paint the post*, which refers to the player shooting overhand. This is important because it protects the stick from being checked more easily in gamelike situations. Midfielders should shoot a three-quarter arm shot and encourage a bounce shot hitting a foot in front of the crease. Balls shot in this manner tend to have a good chance of going in because they can stay low to the ground and bounce waist high or bounce high over the shoulder of the goalie, depending on the playing surface conditions.

Four-Corner Shooting F24

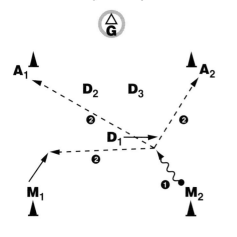

❷ = 3 options to pass

1. Create a grid with the goal centered at one end. Place one marker low left about 10 yards wide of the goal and 5 yards above the crease, another marker low right about 10 yards wide of the goal and 5 yards above the crease, another marker 10 yards wide of the goal and 5 yards inside the restraining line at top left, and the remaining marker 10 yards wide of the goal and 5 yards inside the restraining line at top right. 2. Begin the drill by placing balls at top left with midfielder M2. 3. The three defenders play in a triangle and slide to prevent the offense from scoring. 4. Midfielder M2 begins by attacking toward the goal. 5. Midfielder M2 attacks until defended. If he can attack and get close enough for a high-percentage shot, he should take it; otherwise, he should draw a defender and pass to an open teammate. 6. Play continues until a shot, goal, steal, or save occurs. 7. Play begins again at top left with midfielder M2.

Purpose:
To develop the use of vision to find the best shot possible.
Number of Players:
8 (1 goalie, 2 attackers, 2 midfielders, 3 defenders)
Equipment:
1 goal, 4 field markers, 4 practice jerseys, 4 balls

The ball should stay above the goal line extended. Offensive players are encouraged to work for the *layup*, a shot taken close to the goal, which is usually the easiest and closest shot possible. Defenders work triangle slides and rotate to the recover position; rotation is away from the ball. Players need to communicate with each other about who has the ball and who is sliding to the ball.

Around the World   F25

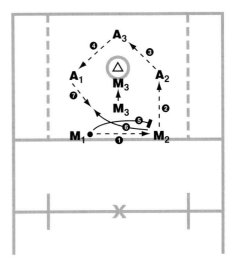

Purpose:
To add shooting to a team offensive formation.
Number of Players:
6 (3 attackers, 3 midfielders)
Equipment:
1 goal, 5 balls

1. Arrange the players as shown in the diagram, in a 2-3-1 formation (see page 44). **2.** All balls begin at top right with midfielder M1. **3.** Midfielder M1 passes to midfielder M2. **4.** M2 passes to attacker A2. **5.** Attacker A2 passes to attacker A3. **6.** A3 passes to attacker A1, who is the feeder. **7.** Attacker A1 enters the feeding zone. **8.** Midfielder M1 picks for midfielder M2, who cuts to the goal toward attacker A1 on a diagonal cut. **9.** Attacker A1 passes to midfielder M2, who shoots. **10.** Midfielder M3 stands about 2 feet off the crease and screens the shot. **11.** Players rotate positions, and play begins again at top right.

This drill presents coaches with a model for adding shooting to a team offensive formation. Other drills are described in the chapter 9, Offensive Drills. Fundamentals of the drill include having players adjacent to the ball execute a V-cut in order to gain space to receive the pass. All feeds should occur on the run. The pick by the top right midfielder should come just outside the opposite goal post. The top right player should pick 2 feet outside the left goal post; this allows the cutting player a better shooting angle once he catches the pass. The shooter should shoot low so that the crease midfielder can screen the shot by allowing it to pass just between or next to his legs, a brave job indeed.

Offensive Drills

This chapter provides drills that break down the concepts of team offense into small parts and progresses to drills that support the whole team functioning successfully on offense. Coaches should design practices that introduce the parts of team offense before players are asked to understand and execute the whole.

     This approach allows players the opportunity to develop the techniques and tactics essential for offensive play without being overwhelmed by complications inherent in whole-team offensive schemes. These complications include reduced vision because of the addition of more players, reduced space for movement because of the addition of more players, reduced time for decision making because of more intense defensive pressure, and more difficulty in communicating between teammates.

     Involving players in drills that are designed to develop offensive technique and tactics such as taking on a defender in a one-on-one situation, recognizing and exploiting a numerical advantage, creating passing lanes for shot opportunities, developing transition skills, maintaining field balance, and developing decision-making and movement skills are essential to the successful team offensive play. After training players using the drills in this chapter to develop these parts of the offense, place your players in more challenging situations by adding more players, as would be appropriate in a whole-team offense.

OFFENSIVE DRILLS

One-on-One to Goal 01

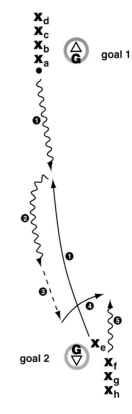

Purpose:
To develop the courage to take on defenders in a one-on-one situation.

Number of Players:
8 to 10 (8 field players, 2 goalies— optional)

Equipment:
2 goals, 10 balls

1. Set up two goals facing each other 20 yards apart. **2.** Have half the players stand with a ball 5 yards to the right of goal 1 and the other half of the players stand with a ball 5 yards to the right of goal 2. **3.** Play begins with a player from the line by goal 1 attacking with a ball toward the opposite goal. **4.** The first player in the other line becomes the defender. **5.** The attacker goes toward the goal until a shot, goal, steal, or save occurs. **6.** If a shot, goal, or save results, the shooter becomes the defender, and the next player from the line by goal 2 begins his attack on goal 1. **7.** If the original play results in a steal, the defender goes toward goal 1 and tries to score. The original attacker now defends. **8.** Play is continuous.

The use of goalies in the drill is optional. Set up specific rules if your team does the drill without goalies. For example, make players cross the halfway point before they can shoot. Place a time limit on the attacking run. (Even if you're using goalies in the drill, you may want a time limit to pick up the tempo of the drill.) Use a shooting net if available. The attacker should be encouraged to attack the middle of the goal. Players who are least comfortable with the drill will tend to drift to the sides and lose their shooting angle. Defenders need to approach the attacker with speed, angle, and distance. The drill emphasizes the role of the first attacker to penetrate, in this case with a dodge and shot.

The drill can be modified and run as a two-on-two to goal. The role of both the second attacker and the second defender is to give support by being in a helping position (see pages 43 and 48).

Three-on-Two to Goal 02

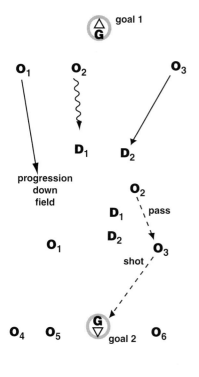

goal 1

O₁   O₂   O₃

D₁   D₂

progression
down
field

O₂

D₁   pass

D₂

O₁   O₃

shot

O₄   O₅   goal 2   O₆

1. Set up two goals 30 yards apart, facing each other. **2.** Players O1, O2, and O3 start from behind goal 1 and attack with the ball toward goal 2. D1 and D2 are the defenders. **3.** O1, O2, and O3 continue until a shot, goal, steal, or save occurs. **4.** If a shot, goal, or save occurs, the shooter (O3) and defenders (D1 and D2) are done. **5.** Play continues with players O4, O5, and O6, starting from behind goal 2, beginning their attack on goal 1 against the two original attackers who didn't shoot (O1 and O2). **6.** If the original play results in a steal, the defender who retrieved the ball (D1 or D2) goes toward goal 1 and tries to score. The original attacker who lost the ball joins the two defenders. All three attack against the remaining two original offensive players (O1 and O2), who now become defenders. **7.** Play is continuous.

Purpose:
To recognize the extra attacker and numerical advantage.

Number of Players:
8 to 10 (8 field players, 2 goalies—optional)

Equipment:
2 goals, 4–6 balls

The effectiveness of the three-on-two relates to spacing. The attackers should have vision of each other at all times and should avoid being in positions where they are in the shadows of the defense, a position that places the defender between them and the ball. In addition, the two players without the ball should be at different levels and in different areas of play so that they aren't easily defended. The player with the ball should be reminded of his role to penetrate the defense. Emphasize that diagonal runs create space for the player with the ball and usually force defenders to make marking decisions. Lateral runs make space for others. It is generally a good idea to set up the three offensive players in a triangle formation with two down low near the goal. This creates the ideal spacing and passing/shooting situations. Since the balls are shot wide or thrown out-of-bounds, it's a good idea to have extra balls on hand so play can continue without interruptions while the balls are retrieved.

OFFENSIVE DRILLS

Feeding Frenzy 03

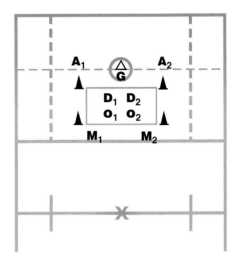

Purpose:
To develop moves to create passing lanes and attack the goal.

Number of Players:
9–13 (1 goalie, 2–4 defenders, 6 offensive players, including 2–4 attackers, 2–4 midfielders)

Equipment:
4 field markers, 10 balls, 6 practice jerseys, 1 goal

1. Create a 20-by-20-yard grid. Place a goal centered on one side and 5 yards outside the grid. **2.** Inside the grid are two defenders, D1 and D2, and two offensive players, O1 and O2. **3.** Outside the grid on the low left of goal and the low right of goal but above the goal line extended are two attackers, A1 and A2. **4.** Opposite the goal and 5 yards outside the grid are two midfielders, M1 and M2. They are 10 yards apart. **5.** Play begins with players M1 and M2 passing the ball back and forth. **6.** Players O1 and O2 use V-cuts to get open. One of the outside midfielders feeds one inside player. The other outside midfielder moves into the grid and helps attack the goal three-on-two. **7.** Play continues until a shot, goal, save, or steal occurs. **8.** The three offensive players inside the grid then balance the grid and look for a feed from the left low offensive player, attacker A2. **9.** Play continues until a shot, goal, save, or steal occurs. **10.** The three players inside then balance the grid and look for a feed from the right low offensive player, attacker A1. **11.** Play continues until a shot, goal, save, or steal occurs. **12.** Once each of the three feeding positions has taken a turn, play begins at the top with the two feeders.

It's important for the top feeding players to catch the ball, change direction, and maintain vision with the inside offensive players. The feed should come on a diagonal pass. This allows the greatest vision for the offensive player receiving the ball and also allows him to shield the ball more effectively. The receiving player is able to rotate his shoulders so that his stick is protected. Inside offensive players should focus on the timing of their cuts to the ball. The feeder must be ready to feed before the run is executed. Low players should be in motion when feeding. They should maintain vision and communicate with the player to help maintain balance inside the grid. Defenders must play behind the inside offensive players until the first pass from the top. This helps the offense work on their cuts. Emphasize to the offensive players inside the grid to work at different levels and distances above the goal. This helps them maintain open spaces and places them in better help positions.

The drill can be modified by adding defenders to pressure A1 and A2 and M1 and M2.

Four-on-Two in Grid 04

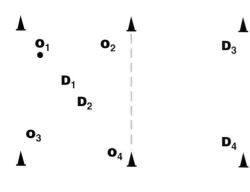

1. Create a 40-by-40-yard grid and divide it in half with a centerline. **2.** Four players from one team begin with the ball on their side of the centerline. Two players from the other team go across the centerline to play defense. **3.** The four offensive players pass the ball between them on their side of the grid until they throw the ball outside the grid or the defense touches or steals a pass. The offensive team gets 1 point for every five successive passes. **4.** Once the offense loses possession, one defender passes across the centerline to his teammates. The two defenders then cross the centerline back to their side and work to maintain possession. The other team sends two players to defend. **5.** Play is continuous.

Purpose:
To develop transition skills.
Number of Players:
8 (4 defenders, 4 offensive players)
Equipment:
6 field markers, 4 practice jerseys, 1 ball

The drill helps with communication, vision, movement, passing, catching, field balance, and transition. Players are encouraged to make quick decisions regarding the transition from offense to defense. Who will play defense? How can we quickly get our passes for points? How can I move to help the team? Use situations like this to help players learn to make better decisions especially related to movement, possession, and field balance.

OFFENSIVE DRILLS

Four-on-Three Field Balance 05

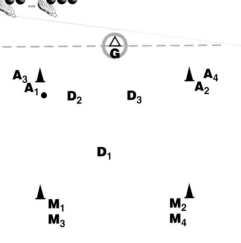

Purpose:
To maintain field balance in order to create shooting opportunities.

Number of Players:
8–12 (1 goalie, 2–4 midfielders, 2–4 attackers, 3 defenders)

Equipment:
1 goal, 4 field markers, 3 practice jerseys, 6 balls

1. Create a 20-by-20-yard grid, with the goal centered on one side about 5 yards outside the grid. **2.** All balls should begin at one of the four markers. **3.** Play begins with the player with the ball attacking the goal and then passing or shooting, depending on how the defense reacts. The purpose is for the offense to maintain possession and pass to earn the best shot possible. **4.** Play continues until a shot, goal, steal, or save occurs. **5.** Play resumes from the same marker for four additional attempts. **6.** Then rotate the balls to a different marker and begin play. Play will occur from all markers.

The player with the ball should attack the goal to draw a defender and then make the best pass or best shot possible. One low attacker should back up any shot taken, and the other low attacker should move to the front of the goal for a rebound. By attacking from all markers, players have the opportunity to learn passing lanes and shooting angles and how they differ in different parts of the offensive zone. Since the balls are shot wide or thrown out-of-bounds, it's a good idea to have extra balls on hand so play can continue without interruptions while the balls are retrieved.

Goalie Game 06

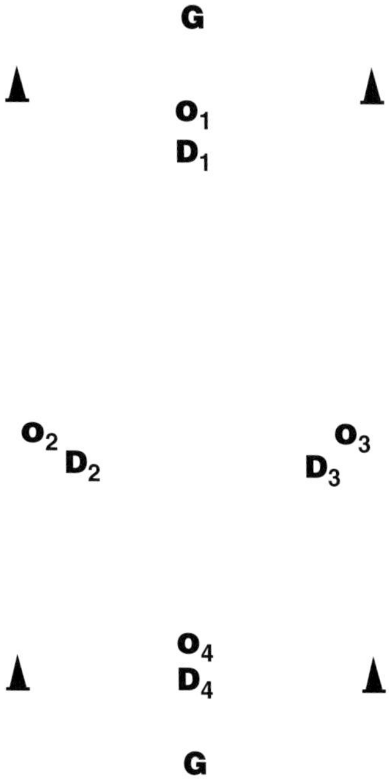

G

▲   **O₁**
            D₁   ▲

O₂   **O₃**
   D₂   **D₃**

▲   **O₄**
            D₄   ▲

G

1. Create a 20-by-40-yard grid. **2.** Two teams of four players are inside the grid, and two goalies are outside the grid at opposite ends. **3.** The object is to move the ball from one goalie to the other by passing inside the grid. **4.** The play begins with one goalie (any player at one end and outside the grid) passing to one team. **5.** This team works to move the ball from the first goalie to the other goalie. **6.** If possession is lost, the defending team passes to their goalie, and play begins in the other direction. **7.** Play is continuous.

Offensive players inside the grid should maintain a diamond shape. Players should stay wide and maintain depth, stretching the space the defenders must cover. Focus on diagonal and lateral movement to open up spaces and to create opportunities to move the ball forward. Defensive players should prevent penetration and should be in a position to help if players get beaten.

Purpose:
To develop offensive decision making and movement skills.
Number of Players:
10 (2 goalies, 4 defenders, 4 offensive players)
Equipment:
4 field markers, 10 practice jerseys (2 colors), 1 ball

OFFENSIVE DRILLS

Four-on-Three Triangle Fast Break 07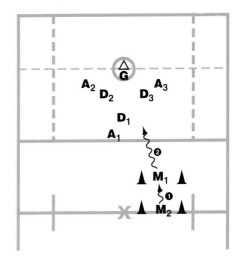

Purpose:
To develop an understanding of how to finish a standard fast break.

Number of Players:
9 (1 goalie, 3 attackers, 3 defenders, 2 midfielders)

Equipment:
1 goal, 4 field markers (for modification), 9 practice jerseys, 6 balls (6 for each side)

1. Play begins at the midfield.
2. Place a goalie in the goal, and three defenders and three attackers inside the restraining line. **3.** Two midfielders will be at the midline or center circle. The play begins with one midfielder scooping a ground ball and creating a fast break. **4.** The midfielder attacks the goal either top left or top right and continues to the goal until one defender slides and takes him.
5. Once the defender has stopped the penetration by the midfielder, the midfielder passes to the point attacker, A1. This is important for maintaining possession and keeping a numerical advantage. **6.** The point attacker must decide to shoot or pass. Play continues until a goal, save, steal, or throwaway (the ball is thrown out of-bounds) occurs. **7.** Begin with a new midfielder.

The midfielder must attack top left or top right to keep team balance. The point attacker must be 3–5 yards inside the restraining line. The low attacker completes the triangle by being 7 yards wide and 5 yards above the goal line extended. This maintains balance. The midfielder passes to the point once the defender has stopped penetration. This should occur on all breaks unless one of the defenders has clearly left his low attacker. If the midfielder isn't covered, then he continues and shoots. The point player's first look is the diagonal to the opposite low attacker. The second look is to the same side attacker or back to the midfielder. The point player should also evaluate the opportunity to shoot by peeking at the defense before the pass is made by the midfielder. The point player should gauge his distance from the goal. Play could also begin with a one-on-one in a grid (see illustration) at midfield. This would simulate a clearing under pressure situation. Also, to simulate a more realistic game situation, have the three attackers and three defenders start at the top of the restraining box and move into position when the play starts.

Full-Field Fast Break 08

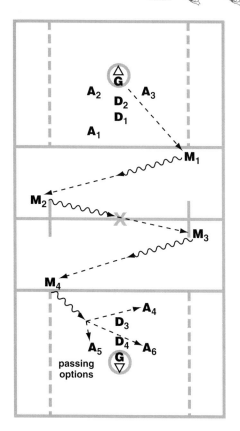

passing options

1. Place a goalie in each goal on a full-size field. Each team has two defenders and three attackers. Other players occupy the midfield positions. **2.** Set four lines of midfielders between the restraining lines with at least two midfielders in each line. Each line is at a different level and about 10 yards from the sideline. **3.** Play begins with the goalie passing to a midfielder who is breaking to the ball. **4.** The receiving midfielder passes diagonally to the next midfielder. This sequence continues until the last midfield line has a four-on-two fast break. **5.** Complete the fast break. Once a shot is taken, the midfielder breaks for a clear pass and begins to play in the other direction. **6.** Midfielders follow their passes to the next line to maintain balance.

Purpose:
To develop the concept of the fast break.
Number of Players:
16 (2 goalies, 4 defenders, 4 midfielders, 6 attackers)
Equipment:
10 balls (5 in each goal), practice jerseys (5–10)

This drill creates a fast-paced full-transition model. The object is to execute a fast transition to the offensive zone and finish with a four-on-two. Midfielders are aligned on diagonals. This type of cutting or motion is best for creating *attacking lanes* (space used or created for a player to dodge to a goal or advance the ball up the field) and moving the ball quickly up the field. All midfielders are encouraged to make a V-cut in order to gain space and position before they make the diagonal cut. The defense is then forced to make a difficult play. The advantage is with the offense in order to encourage finishing in transition. The defense must use a *stack slide*: Defensive players begin in a stack. The first defender picks up the midfielder 5 yards inside the restraining line. The second player remains in the middle, splitting the offensive players and waiting for the first pass. Once the pass is made, the second defender goes to the pass, and the first defender replaces him. The object is for the defense to recover to the middle as quickly as possible and force an outside shot.

OFFENSIVE DRILLS

Scramble Five-on-Four 09

Purpose:
To develop attacking techniques and tactics in an extra-player offense.

Number of Players:
10 (1 goalie, 2 midfielders, 3 attackers, 4 defenders)

Equipment:
1 goal, 5 balls

1. Create a 30-by-30-yard grid with the goal centered on one side 5 yards outside the grid. **2.** All offensive and defensive players begin outside the grid. The crease player, A3, begins at any marker. **3.** You or an assistant start the play from any location with a throw or ground ball to any offensive player. **4.** Play goes five-on-four to goal, or five-on-five with a clear to you if the defense steals the pass or gets a ground ball.

One offensive player occupies the crease and should move between the high and low post. When the ball is high, he should play low. The crease player can serve as a screen and then work the diagonals to receive a pass. Outside players can move and exchange with the crease player or set a pick for him. The crease player can do the same for the outside players, especially since he can move in the blind spot of the defenders. Maintain balance; don't allow one player to defend two players by moving to closed space or occupying the same area as another offensive player. Players should read their defender. Explain to them that if their defender turns his back to them, this is a great time to cut. The offense should push the ball quickly and have good, quick ball movement. Slowing the drill down will allow the defense to recover. This will help keep the defense moving and create lanes. The offense should draw a defender to create a two-on-one situation. Keep the ball above the goal line extended. Attackers should remain 7 yards wide and 5 yards above the goal line extended. This will create good shooting angles. Defenders should use box slides or rotation slides (see page 49) in this drill. The type of slide depends on the type of team defense your team plays or what you're emphasizing at the time, either player-to-player or zone defense. Defenders want to push the clear quickly to gain an immediate advantage. Players should remember the goalie is available. One defender should watch the *hole*, the area in front of the crease, in case of a turnover.

Six-on-Five Slow Break 010

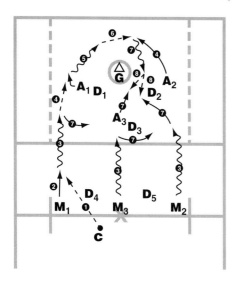

1. Space three offensive midfielders (M1, M2, and M3) across the midfield. Begin at the midfield with a three-on-two ground ball directed toward one of the midfielders. **2.** On the start, a defensive midfielder (D4 or D5) attempts to get the ball, but he shouldn't overplay the situation and should work to remain in a position to recover. **3.** Offensive midfielders work to move the ball down the side. **4.** The ball moves down a side through the attack to point behind. **5.** The player at point behind, A2, drives the ball up the *weak side* (the side of the field without the ball), hitting either the crease attacker or the midfielder cutting on the weak side. **6.** The play continues until the offensive players take a shot or lose possession of the ball. The drill can end at this point and then resume with a new group of midfielders, or the goalie can initiate a clear to the defending midfielders.

Purpose:
To recognize the difference between full-field transition and odd player situations that develop more slowly or in the half-field situation.
Number of Players:
12 (1 goalie, 3 attackers, 3 midfielders, 5 defenders)
Equipment:
12 practice jerseys, 10 balls

The midfielders should push the ball quickly down the side. It's important for the weak-side midfielder to time his run down the back side. If the midfielder is too early, the defense can slide or cover two players, and the slow break or transition is lost. The crease attacker should maintain a high post until the player at the point behind is in the feeding zone and ready to pass. It's important to work the ball quickly to the weak side. The crease attacker should stay in a high post crease. He begins the V-cut 12 yards above the goal and explodes to the front. Not only does this give the cutting player an opportunity to score, but it allows a space behind the cutter to open for the center midfielder to fill. The midfielders need to maintain balance, so they should fill these areas. One midfielder is the weak-side or back-side cutter. The center midfielder assumes the high crease about 12 yards above the goal. The third midfielder rotates across the top to back up any feed from behind to the cutting midfielder or crease (15 to 18 yards above the goal). This also prevents the other team from making a fast break.

Full-Field Scramble 011

Purpose:
To develop the conditioning needed to make the transition from offense to defense (a transition game) and to recognize the quickly changing conditions of a transition game.

Number of Players:
20 (2 goalies, 6 attackers, 6 midfielders, 6 defenders)

Equipment:
2 goals, 10 or 20 practice jerseys, 10 balls (at the midfield and in each goal)

1. Start on a full-size field with a goalie in each goal, three defenders and three offensive players at each end, and a coach and six midfielders at the midfield sideline. **2.** The drill starts with a one-on-one ground ball from you or an assistant coach. The players battle for the loose ball, and the player who gains possession continues and leads a four-on-three fast break. **3.** Play continues until a steal or shot occurs. On a steal, the ball goes to the goalie; on a save, the goalie begins the play in the opposite direction by calling "clear." **4.** Two midfielders are then released from the midfield and move back to the goal to aid in the clear. The goalie is free to play the ball to a defender or to the midfielders cutting to the ball. The midfielders must cut below the restraining line before they may receive the pass. **5.** The play continues in the opposite direction with a five-on-four fast break. **6.** Play continues until a steal or save occurs. The goalie then initiates the clear, and two players from the original fast-breaking team (the four-on-three) are released from the midfield and must cut below the restraining line before they can receive a pass. **7.** Continue until the drill reaches six-on-six for one full field in each direction.

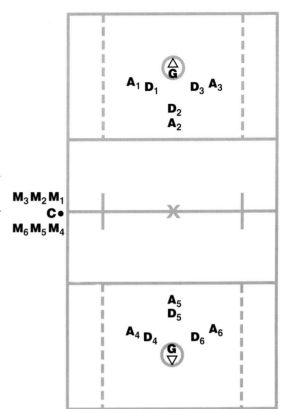

The focus of this drill is on the diagonal pass and spacing. Players need to use the diagonal cut to create lanes for pushing the ball quickly up the field. Defenders should use the *J-cut*, where the defender breaks from the low defensive position to the outside, to get wide and open up lanes for clearing.

The drill plays out three types of transition and advantage situations: the four-on-three, the five-on-four, and the six-on-five. In the four-on-three and five-on-four situations the attacking team should keep the ball above the goal line extended. In the six-on-five situation the ball can go behind in order to take advantage of the weak-side or back-side cutter. Defensively, teams are forced to work on recovery and should understand the importance of staying involved in the play. In the four-on-three situation the defense should work the triangle slides. In the five-on-four situation the defense should work the rotation or box slides. Goalies are encouraged to quickly initiate the clear and to look first to the defender who was guarding the shooter, especially from the midfield.

CHAPTER 10

Defensive Drills

This chapter provides drills that break down the concepts of team defense into small parts and progresses to drills that support the whole team functioning successfully as a defensive unit. Coaches should design practices that introduce the parts of team defense before players are asked to understand and execute the whole.

This approach allows players the opportunity to develop the techniques and tactics essential for defensive play without being overwhelmed by complications inherent in whole-team defensive schemes.

Shuttle Run D1

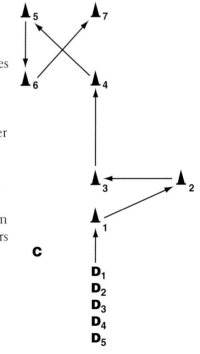

Purpose:
To develop defensive footwork.

Number of Players:
5

Equipment:
7 field markers

1. Begin by placing the field markers approximately 5–8 yards apart at various angles as pictured in the diagram. **2.** The drill begins at marker 1, and players proceed in sequential order. **3.** Player D1 begins by running diagonally from marker 1 to marker 2. **4.** The player then moves laterally from marker 2 to marker 3 by shuffling his feet and maintaining the proper defensive position. **5.** At marker 3 the player executes a drop step and *back-pedals* (runs backward in a low stance with the head up and shoulders square) to marker 4. **6.** From marker 4 the player again moves diagonally to marker 5. **7.** When the player reaches marker 5 he sprints forward to marker 6. **8.** At marker 6 the player completes the drill by moving diagonally to marker 7.

The diagonal movement of the player should occur with his shoulders square to the coach, who is standing near the line of defensive players, and with the stick out in front, so the player is ready to react to a pass, ground ball, or checking opportunity. The player should use a normal running motion to move diagonally. This allows him to close the most space in the fastest possible way. Moving laterally requires the defensive player to shuffle his feet. This is done with his feet and shoulders square to the coach. The feet can be slightly offset so that the player can perform a *drop step* when needed or explode diagonally or forward to slide, intercept a pass, or win a ground ball. Players perform a drop step at markers 3 and 6 by swinging their lead foot backward a greater distance than a normal step, and allowing their hips to face the new direction of the defensive movement. At marker 5 the forward sprint is completed and simulates the defender's need to close the space as quickly as possible. This occurs with a normal running motion. All changes of direction are made with the defender leading with his stick. By moving the stick in the direction of the play, the defender can transfer weight more effectively. It's also important for the defender to keep his eyes forward, but he can sneak a quick look to locate the next marker. Use this drill as part of station work. If all defenders and midfielders are involved in this drill at the same time, provide two sets of markers to prevent players standing in long lines.

Foot Fire D2

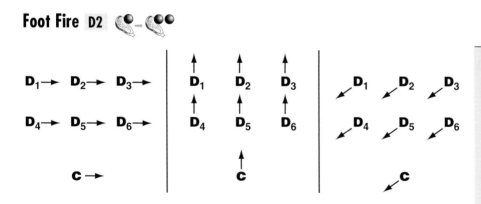

Purpose:
To develop proper body and stick position and the ability to change direction more effectively.

Number of Players:
6

Equipment:
None

1. Begin by placing two rows of defenders with at least a stick's length of space between them in all directions. **2.** When you give the "foot fire" command, players react by moving their feet rapidly as if running in place. **3.** With the next command, "break down," players assume proper defensive position, their stick in front and their eyes up and scanning. **4.** All players then move in the direction you point. **5.** Players can also face each other in this drill. Instead of moving in the same direction, each player would mirror his partner and critique his defensive positioning and movement.

The ability to develop and improve quickness is important for defenders. Quite often they are playing against the quickest players on the field, the attackers. Drills that emphasize proper positioning and movement are essential for success. Proper positioning includes players being on the balls of their feet, with the feet about shoulder-width apart and slightly offset. The offset angle helps force an attacker one direction and makes the attacking player more predictable. Stick position includes the arms slightly extended with the bottom hand on the end of the stick and the top hand positioned a comfortable distance above the bottom hand. The bottom hand should be about waist high and the top hand slightly higher. The drop step is used to begin movement in a backward direction and to help the defensive player maintain or establish an angle of defense. Use this drill as part of station work. Include attackers because of their necessity to play defense when *riding*, or trying to prevent the defense from clearing the ball.

One-on-One in Grid D3

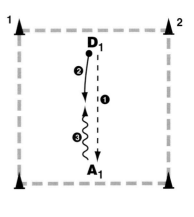

Purpose:
To develop the fundamentals of individual defense.
Number of Players:
2 (1 defender, 1 offensive player)
Equipment:
1 ball, 4 field markers

1. Establish a 10-by-10-yard grid. **2.** The defensive player begins with the ball and passes to the offensive player. The defensive player's job is to prevent the offensive player from dodging or running the ball across the defender's grid line (the space between markers 1 and 2). **3.** Once the offensive player (the attacker) catches the pass, the defender may leave his line and begin playing defense. **4.** Play ends when the attacker successfully makes it across the line, or when the defender forces the attacker outside the grid or is able to check the ball away.

The defender should approach the attacker with concern for speed, angle, and distance. *Speed* simply means he should approach as fast as possible. The *angle* taken is a curved run, like that of a banana (also known as a banana run). This is done to eliminate the possibility for the attacker to dodge in both directions. *Distance* refers to the defender reaching a comfortable distance from the attacker, breaking down and maintaining his cushion. Caution the defender to be patient and to allow the attacker to make the mistake. The defender should use his stick and its length to his advantage. If the attacker changes directions, the defender should use the drop step to maintain his cushion, or the distance between himself and the attacker. Set up several grids so that more than two players can participate at the same time.

Two-on-Two in Grid D4

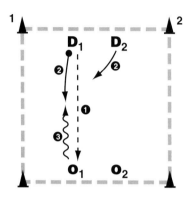

1. Establish a 15-by-15-yard grid. **2.** Play begins with the defensive pair passing to the offensive pair. **3.** Once one of the offensive players catches the pass, the defensive pair leaves their line and works together to prevent the offensive pair from dodging or passing across the defensive line (between markers 1 and 2). **4.** One defender assumes the role of the first defender and closes with speed, angle, and distance. The other defender becomes the second defender and gives support at an angle. **5.** Play ends when the offensive player successfully makes it across the defensive line, when the defenders force the offensive player outside the grid, or when the defenders are able to check the ball away.

Purpose:
To develop the role of the second defender.
Number of Players:
4 (2 defenders, 2 offensive players)
Equipment:
1 ball, 4 field markers

The role of the first defender is to stop penetration by the offensive team. He defends with speed, angle, and distance. The second defender provides support for the first defender. His role is to be in a position to cover a passing lane and to slide if the first defender is beaten by a dodge. The second defender should be at a 45-degree angle behind the first defender and on the same side as the second offensive player. His stick position should be up at a 45-degree angle and in the passing lane covering just behind the first defender. If the second offensive player moves behind the first offensive player and the ball is passed to him, the second defender would call a switch, and the first defender would step through to the player with the ball. If the second offensive player cuts diagonally in behind the first defender, the second defender follows the cutter and tells the first defender to change his angle of defense in order to force the offensive player with the ball toward the help side. Certain situations such as the first offensive player failing to pass the ball as the second offensive player cuts behind him would allow for opportunities to double-team the ball. As a change of pace, there can be an automatic double-team when you blow the whistle. This gives the defenders practice at double-teaming and the offensive players practice at handling pressure and finding the open player.

Stack-Slide Pressure Cooker D5

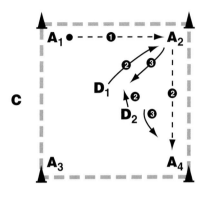

Purpose:
To develop the technique of the stack slide and of recovering to the hole to provide support.

Number of Players:
6 (2 defenders, 4 attackers)

Equipment:
1 ball, 4 field markers

1. Establish a 10-by-10-yard grid. **2.** One attacker, A1, begins with the ball and makes a pass to player A2. The two defenders begin in the middle of the grid in proper defensive stance and react to the first pass to begin play. **3.** The first defender begins the stack slide by closing on the ball with speed, angle, and distance. The second defender remains near the middle, taking the opposite angle of defense, and has his stick up and in the lane to block a pass. **4.** The second attacker passes to another attacker to continue the drill. **5.** The defenders respond by changing roles. The player in the middle approaches this pass with speed, angle, and distance. The second player recovers to the middle and takes the opposite angle of defense with his stick up and in the lane to steal a pass.
6. Play continues for several passes; the players change roles and repeat the drill.

Defending players must assume their roles quickly and communicate angle of defense, which makes the next pass more predictable. If the defender can force the next pass back toward the original passer, it will help place pressure on the offensive team because usually the greatest defensive pressure is where the ball has just been. Recovery to the middle for the defense begins with the stick movement to the direction of recovery and with the drop step. Once the change of direction has occurred, the defensive player should keep his stick up and in a passing lane, should have his eyes up, and should be communicating the angles of defense.

Circle One-on-One to Goal D6 🥍– 🥍●●●

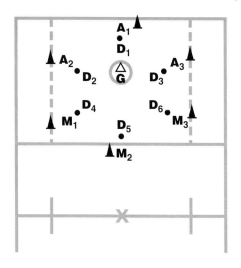

1. Establish the field markers at the dodging stations located in the diagram. **2.** Play begins on your whistle or command from a designated point. **3.** One dodge occurs at a time. **4.** The offensive player with the ball is given 5 seconds to dodge to the goal. **5.** The defender's job is to prevent the player from dodging and taking a shot. **6.** Play ends with a shot, goal, or steal by the defender, or time running out. **7.** Continue the drill with a new offensive player trying to dodge his defender.

Purpose:
To develop the concept of defensive positioning according to the location of the ball.

Number of players:
13 (1 goalie, 6 defenders, 6 offensive players— 3 attackers, 3 midfielders)

Equipment:
1 goal, 6 balls, 6 field markers, 6 practice jerseys

All defenders should choose an angle of defense as play begins. The defender dictates where the offensive player is going to go. The defender at point behind and the defender at top center choose the angle of defense that fits their team's scheme of defending. For newer players or if your team doesn't have a scheme yet, the player should angle the way he's most comfortable defending. Defenders of offensive players located on the sides should take an angle of defense that forces the player toward point behind. Defenders playing the top left or right offensive player should take an angle of defense that forces the players wide and reduces the shooting angle. Defending from point behind is difficult because the defender has to change angle of defense. As the offensive player reaches the goal line extended, the defender should use the crease to his advantage and force the offensive player toward the crease or back toward point behind. Using the crease is also useful for side defenders in this drill. The goalie's role is to communicate angles of defense and to give location on the field, such as point behind, goal line extended, top left, top right, left behind, right behind, or center front.

DEFENSIVE DRILLS

Four-Corner Slide D7

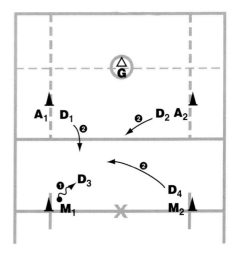

Purpose:
To develop sliding techniques and communication between defenders.

Number of Players:
9 (1 goalie, 4 defenders, 4 offensive players—
2 attackers, 2 midfielders)

Equipment:
1 goal, 5 balls, 4 field markers

1. Establish a 30-by-30-yard grid centered in a half field about 5 yards above the goal line extended and with the goal centered in relation to the grid. **2.** The field markers serve as points for beginning play. The offensive player at each marker should have a ball. **3.** Play begins with any offensive player you or the goalie designates. The offensive player attacks the goal. **4.** His defender plays passively but is allowed to throw one check. **5.** The offensive player continues the dodge. **6.** The remaining three defenders and the goalie must communicate the slides that are needed to prevent the attacking player from scoring or passing to one of the other offensive players who are also active and involved in the play. **7.** Play continues until a shot, goal, steal, or save occurs, and then play begins again with another offensive player at one of the other field markers.

The first defender must establish an angle of defense even though he is playing passively. This helps the goalie and other defenders determine which player will slide. If play begins at top right and the defender D1 is dodged to the outside toward low right, the low defender D3 must slide toward top right with speed, maintaining the proper angle to force the offensive player to the outside, lead with the stick, and follow through with the shoulder if a body check is needed. It's important for defender D3 to anticipate the dodge and be in position so the offensive player doesn't gain too much space. Defender D4 must slide across the face of the goal from low left to low right in order to help defender D3. This is the second slide. Defender D2 must move from top left to low left and is responsible for players A2 and M2.

If the dodge comes to the inside of defender D1, defender D2 must slide to help. Defender D4 must slide down (toward the goal), and defender D3 is responsible for splitting players M1 and M2. For low defensive play, if defender D3 is beaten to the inside, defender D4 must slide across the goal, defender D2 must slide up (toward the restraining line) to cover player M2, and defender D1 is responsible for players A1 and A2. If defender D3 is beaten to the outside, defender D1 slides up, defender D2 slides over, and defender D4 is responsible for players A2 and M2.

Communication, anticipation, and proper fundamentals (speed, angle, distance) are essential to successful sliding. It's also important that defenders slide to their proper offensive players with their sticks up and in the passing lane.

Four-on-Three Defensive Possession D8

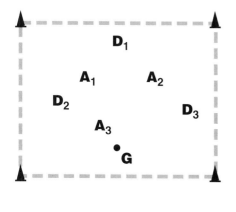

1. Create a 30-by-30-yard grid. **2.** Inside the grid are two or three attackers or midfielders serving as a riding team (defensive role). **3.** Also inside the grid are three or four defenders and a goalie, who serve as the clearing team (offensive role). **4.** Play begins with the goalie on the clearing team passing the ball to a teammate. **5.** Once the first pass is made, the riding team works to steal the ball and the clearing team works to maintain possession. **6.** The riding team should focus on moving into open space to receive a pass from a teammate. **7.** Play is restricted to the grid.

Movement by the defenders will depend on the presure. The goal is to try to maintain the diamond shape shown above. However, it may be necessary for one of the defenders or the goalie to move to the center to be in a better help position.

The object is to help the defenders develop stick skills, vision, and communication needed to effectively clear the ball under pressure and begin the transition game. This is a game of keep away, a great drill for the long-stick defenders to work on their off hand and to develop stick control and protection with the ball, since space is limited.

Purpose:
To develop passing and movement skills needed for starting the transition game in the defensive end.
Number of Players:
6–8 (1 goalie, 3–4 defenders, 2–3 attackers or midfielders)
Equipment:
4 field markers, 2 balls, 3 practice jerseys

Five-on-Four Defensive Pressure D9

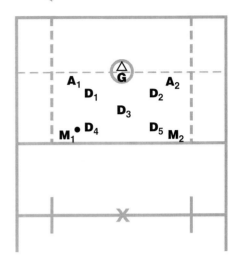

Purpose:
To develop the help and recovery defensive tactic used in double-teaming situations.

Number of Players:
10 (1 goalie, 5 defenders, 2 attackers, 2 midfielders)

Equipment:
1 goal, 5 balls

1. Organize the players as shown in the diagram. The attackers should be at least 7 yards wide of the goal and 5 yards above the goal line extended. Midfielders should be just inside the restraining line to start. Defensive pressure may force the attacker wider or the midfielder higher. **2.** Begin with one offensive player in possession of the ball. A defender marks all offensive players, playing in proper ball-side and goal-side position. **3.** The offense works to score and maintain possession. **4.** The defenders, who are in a 2 1 2 formation, work together to prevent the offense from scoring. The crease defender has no player to mark in this drill. He is free to double-team the ball. **5.** Play continues until a shot, goal, steal, or save occurs. Play restarts with a throw from the goalie to an offensive player. You might blow your whistle to force a doubling. This will increase the tempo of the drill and give players more practice with double-teaming, sliding, and offensive passing against pressure.

Maintaining proper defensive position is important. However, the defenders in this drill are encouraged to play very aggressively because they know they have a helper. Defenders should try to maintain proper angle of defending, which allows for easier double-teams. The goalie or crease defender should initiate the double-team, or you might do so. Communication between players is important. Once the double-team opportunity is lost, one of the doubling defenders must return to the crease to be in the help position, and the other must maintain his position on the offensive player. When returning to the crease area, the player should keep an eye on where the ball is or listen as the goalie communicates this information. This drill will help teams that decide to slide from the crease, teams that play with a designated help defender, or teams that play zone defense.

Fast-Break Triangle Slides D10

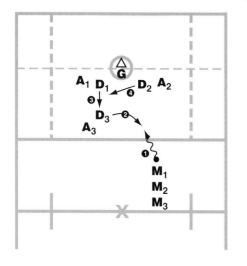

1. Offensive players will set up in a traditional fast-break form: attacker A1 is the point, attacker A2 the low right, and attacker A3 the low left. **2.** The defenders begin in a marking position. **3.** The play begins with a midfielder attacking the goal beginning 10 yards outside the restraining line. **4.** When the midfielder attacks a side, the defenders are forced to leave the attackers they're marking in order to prevent the attacking midfielder from scoring. **5.** Defender D1 becomes the point defender; defenders D2 and D3 complete the triangle at low right and low left. **6.** Defender D1 plays the midfielder about 5 yards inside the restraining line. **7.** Defender D2 or D3 reacts to the next pass and slides accordingly. **8.** All defensive players recover to the triangle once their player passes the ball. **9.** Play continues until a shot, goal, steal, or save occurs. Play begins with a new midfielder.

Purpose:
To develop the slide technique used when defending.
Number of Players:
10 (1 goalie, 3 defenders, 3 attackers, 3 midfielders)
Equipment:
1 goal, 5 balls

It's important for the defense to stay compact. Expanding the triangle creates larger passing lanes and allows the offensive players to make easier decisions and have more time and space to make those decisions. Defensive players should keep their stick in the passing lanes when recovering and should lead with their stick when moving to defend a player with the ball. As the defender approaches, he should try to put stick on stick to intercept a pass or attack the hand to disrupt the pass. This is a great drill for teaching defensive rotation and communication and can be used when teaching player-down defense. To add more game reality to the drill, have offensive and defensive players start at top or inside restraining boxes (or both) and run in to the break formations when the drill starts.

DEFENSIVE DRILLS

Team Defense   D11

Purpose:
To develop team defensive movement and communication.
Number of Players:
13 (1 goalie, 6 defenders, 3 attackers, 3 midfielders)
Equipment:
1 goal, 5 balls

1. Arrange your team around the goal as shown in the diagram. The offense is in a three-on-three formation, in which each defensive player marks an offensive player. **2.** Play begins with the offense, which simply passes the ball on your command or whistle. **3.** Work with the defense on each pass to determine proper defensive angles and player positioning between the ball and the goal. **4.** Once the defensive players are comfortable with the format and understand their slide responsibilities, you can allow

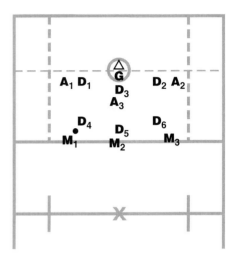

the offense to play at game speed. **5.** Play continues until a shot, goal, steal, or save occurs, or until you stop play to show players how a certain move should be performed. Play begins again with a pass from the goalie.

The focus is on defensive positioning and the defender's ability to adjust to the ball movement. In order to play good team defense, all players must understand the proper terminology and their roles. You can use this drill to teach team slides or special defenses. Several modifications are helpful once the drill is understood. You can have the offense pass the ball until you blow the whistle. At that time the offensive player dodges to the goal. The defender allows the offensive player to go, and the team must slide. The defender who got dodged can practice getting into the hole, or crease, after he gets dodged. Have him count to three, and then rush into the crease area and look for the open offensive player. Then the defense can readjust after the sixth defender finds his new offensive player. The offense can also change formations to help the defense adjust to various offensive schemes. Being able to recognize the need for defensive adjustment and how to adjust shows that your team is really beginning to understand how to play team defense.

Defensive Clearing D12

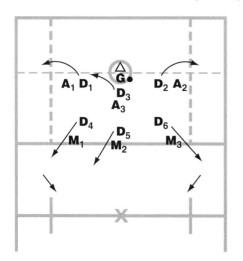

1. Players are organized in a six-on-six half-field game. **2.** The offensive team begins with the ball. **3.** The offense works the ball and tries to score. **4.** On your whistle the offense passes or shoots to the goalie. **5.** The defensive players break to their clearing positions when the goalie calls "break." **6.** Play continues until you whistle or until the defense clears the ball past midfield. Play begins again on the goalie's pass to the offense.

Purpose:
To develop the tactic of how to initiate transition on a turnover.
Number of Players:
13 (1 goalie, 3 defenders, 6 midfielders, 3 attackers)
Equipment:
1 goal, 5 balls

The drill should first be taught without any offensive players. The ball begins with the goalie, and the defensive players respond to his "break" call. Players execute their clearing runs, and the goalie initiates the clear. Then add a full complement of offensive players once clearing responsibilities are understood.

Two low defenders have the responsibility of breaking to the sidelines by making a J-cut or banana run. These players should stay even or slightly behind the ball to maintain vision with the goalie. The crease defender is responsible for the hole and should move about 10 yards to the left or right of the goalie. The top right or left midfielders should break out and up the field on diagonals. It's easier for the goalie to judge the distance of the pass if the player is moving diagonally. Moving straight up the field is much more difficult to read in order to make an effective pass. The center midfielder should cut toward one side on a diagonal, or move diagonally away from a defender or teammate to open space, or find a passing lane.

Once your players understand how to move and maintain vision on the ball, changes can be made to the drill. One rule many teams follow is that when a midfielder shoots, the marking midfielder immediately breaks so that he gains space and can start a fast break in the other direction. He returns to play defense if the goalie or a defensive player does not have possession. Understanding clearing responsibilities will help your players in creating a great transition game. Also, if there are four long-stick defenders on the field, the fourth one should break toward the substitution box so that you can substitute a short-stick defender for a smoother transition to the offense.

APPENDIX: Referee Signals

1. Time-out for discretionary or injury time-out. Follow signal above with tapping of hands on chest

2. Score

3. No score

4. Face-off

5. Out-of-bounds direction of play

6. Loose ball

7. Holding

8. Warding off

9. Stalling

10. Offside

11. Crease violation

12. Illegal body check

Illustration courtesy National Federation of State High School Associations

13. Slashing

14. Cross checking

15. Tripping

16. Unnecessary roughness

17. Unsportsmanlike conduct

18. Play-on. Dead ball or dead ball followed by appropiate foul signal

Sample Scorebook Page

PLACE: _North Harford High_
DATE: _April 12 2000_
REFEREE: _Mr. Smith_
UMPIRE: _Mr. Jones_
FIELD JUDGE: _Mr. Adams_

TEAM: _North Harford Hawks_
Time of Quarters: _10_ Min
1:58

TIME OUT	X	2	3	4	1 ov.	2 ov.

Roster

Position	No.	Name	Q1	Q2	Q3	Q4
ATTACK	16	Tim Flottemesch	✓	✓	✓	✓
ATTACK	10	Adam Pistel	✓	✓	✓	✓
ATTACK	12	Dan Petty	✓	✓	✓	✓
MIDFIELD	6	Sean Noonan	✓	✓	✓	✓
MIDFIELD	9	Matt Pollhammer	✓	✓	✓	
MIDFIELD	24	Mike Bedsaul	✓	✓	✓	✓
DEFENSE	14	Greg Grimm	✓	✓	✓	
DEFENSE	11	Doug Testerman	✓	✓	✓	
DEFENSE	2	Matt Edie	✓	✓	✓	
Goal	1	Andrew Bonghart	✓	✓		
M 2nd MIDFIELD	7	Mike Taylor	✓	✓	✓	
M 2nd MIDFIELD	29	Mark Kamysiak	✓	✓	✓	✓
M 2nd MIDFIELD	15	Drew Kiniry	✓	✓	✓	
A	20	Linsee Lane			✓	✓
A	23	Chad Rigdon			✓	✓
M	3	Nate Lucky	✓	✓	✓	✓
S M	5	Greg Spacek			✓	✓
U M	19	Greg McCallum			✓	✓
B D	18	Eric Rose			✓	✓
S D	21	Charlie Martin	✓	✓	✓	✓
T D	26	Pete Zazzali			✓	✓
I G	22	Matt Burgess			✓	✓
T U M	8	Brian Feindt			✓	✓

Penalties

P-T	No.	Infraction	Per.	Time
:30	7	Pushing	1	7:09
1:00	24	Slashing	1	4:10
:30	9	Holding	2	6:03
1:00	22	Slashing	4	4:05

Saves

	1st half	SAVES 2nd half	Overtime
	|||	₮₮	
	3	5	0

Scoring Summary

No.	Name	Goals	Assists
7	Mike Taylor	7	—
10	Adam Pistel	1	8
3	Nate Lucky	1	—
8	Brian Feindt	1	—
20	Linsee Lane	—	1
9	Matt Pollhammer	1	—
15	Drew Kiniry	1	—
16	Tim Flottemesch	2	—
29	Mark Kamysiak	—	1

Scoring

Score	Goal By	Assist	Per.	Time
1	7	10	1	:26
2	7	29	2	8:25
3	7	10	2	6:27
4	15	10	2	5:05
5	16	—	2	3:46
6	7	10	2	1:23
7	7	10	2	:23
8	7	10	3	7:15
9	10	9	3	5:12
10	3	—	3	5:04
11	9	10	3	4:31
12	7	—	3	1:46
13	16	10	4	9:35
14	8	20	4	7:40
15				
16				
17				
18				
19				
20				
21				
22				
23				
24				
25				
26				
27				
28				
29				
30				

Glossary

Attackers: The three attacking players who play on the offensive half of the field. These are the players who pass, score, and set up goals.

Attacking lane: Lane used by the team in possession of the ball to dodge to the goal or move the ball up the field in transition.

Back side: See *weak side*.

Ball-side: The side of the field that has the ball.

Banana run: An angled defensive run (shaped like a banana) that limits offensive passing, dodging, or shooting.

Body check: Making intentional contact with an opponent using your shoulder. Contact must occur when the opponent is within 5 yards of the ball and must be made from the front, above the knees, and below the neck of the opponent.

Box area: The area by the player's head and above the shoulder. The stick is carried in this position to help protect the stick. It's also the area used to begin the pass and shot, and it's the ideal area to receive a pass.

Box slide: Defensive slides that teach the help position in zone defenses and certain player-down situations.

Catching: To receive a pass or intercept a pass using your stick.

Center front: The position at the top of the restraining box directly in front of the goal.

Centerline: The midfield line that divides the lacrosse field in half.

Checking: Using the stick or body to make legal contact with an opposing player or his stick.

Clamp: A face-off technique using the player's quickness to rotate the head of the stick over top the ball, trapping it underneath the head of the stick.

Clear: A play executed by the defensive team where they effectively run or pass the ball from the defensive half of the field to the offensive half of the field.

Cradling: Using the arms and wrists to keep the ball in the pocket of the stick. Helps a player run while maintaining possession of the ball.

Crease: A 9-foot circle around each goal that creates a buffer around the goalie. Offensive players are prohibited from entering this area, although their sticks may reach inside the crease.

Cross check: A personal foul occurring when a player uses the shaft of the stick to check an opponent.

Cushion: The space between an offensive and defensive player. The defender should be close enough to stick check without lunging, but not so close as to lose his positional advantage between the player with the ball and the goal.

Cutting: Movement by the offensive players off the ball that helps create space for the player or a teammate. Diagonal cuts create opportunities for players to move toward the goal for scoring chances. Lateral cuts help open spaces for teammates.

Defenders: The players who play on the defensive half of the field.

Dodges: Individual moves executed by the first attacker that aid in the role of penetrating. The attacker feints in one direction in an attempt to have the opponent shift his position, and then the attacker quickly changes direction to an open space.

Double-team: A situation where two players defend one player. Usually used on the player with the ball in an attempt to gain possession.

Drop step: A backward step taken to help a defender maintain his cushion or to regain his defensive position.

End lines: The out-of-bounds lines that mark the ends of the field behind each goal.

Extra-player offense: A one-player advantage for the offense gained by a penalty committed by the opposing team.

Face dodge: An individual move executed by moving the stick across the face from one side to the other while penetrating the defense.

Face-off: The special situation that begins the game and is used to start each quarter and to restart the game after a goal. It requires special one-on-one skills to gain possession of the ball.

Fast break: A scoring opportunity created by the transition game giving the offense a player advantage during the regular game play.

Feeding: Passing the ball to a player who catches and shoots on goal.

Feeding zone: An area on each side of the goal used by offensive players to feed other offensive players. It begins about 5 yards from point behind and extends to approximately 10 yards above the goal line extended and 7–10 yards from the goal.

First attacker: The player with the ball. His job is to penetrate to the goal.

First defender: The defensive player marking the player with the ball. His job is to prevent penetration.

Goal: The 6-by-6-foot frame into which teams try to shoot the ball. It is defended by the goalie.

Goalie: The player who has the responsibility of defending the goal by preventing shots from crossing the goal line. He's also responsible for communicating to the defense and beginning the transition game.

Goal line: The line extending from goal post to goal post. The line is used to determine is a goal has been scored. The ball must cross the line entirely for the shot to qualify as a goal.

Goal line extended: An imaginary line that's an extension of the goal line. It's used as a reference for defenders to apply pressure and deny penetration and as a reference for attacking players as a line to reach in order to execute a dodge and have a shooting angle.

Goal-side: When a defender is between his opponent and the goal.

Ground ball: A loose ball. Getting possession of ground balls is a crucial skill.

Head: The plastic portion of the stick extending from the shaft.

Help and recovery: When a player moves to a position to help a teammate and then returns (recovers) back to his original position.

Help position: The supporting defensive position taken by the second defender or attacker, who's at an angle from the first defender or attacker, ready to slide if needed and occupying a passing lane.

Help side: See *help position*.

Holding: An infraction that can be a technical foul or change of possession, depending on whether the holding occurred when the opposing team had possession of the ball. The infraction occurs when the player uses the stick to prevent an opposing player from cutting or dodging.

Hold position: A legal technique used to deny penetration by the defense. If the defender loses his *cushion* (the space between himself and the offensive player), the hold is used to slow the defender's penetration and regain the player's cushion.

Hole: The area in the defensive half of the field in front of the crease area.

Interference: A technical foul that occurs when a defender off the ball prevents a cutter from completing a cut or who prevents a player without the ball from moving.

J-cut: A run executed by a defender breaking from the low defensive position to the outside for a clearing pass. The run is curved so that the player maintains vision with the goalie and ends by curling upfield near the sideline.

Layup: A shot taken close to the goal, usually within five yards.

Left behind: A position behind the goal to the goalie's left.

Long stick: A stick of 52 to 72 inches used primarily by defenders or midfielders.

Man-ball communication: Used by players to identify which player will get the loose ground ball and which player will shield the ball.

Midfielders: The three players who play in both the offensive and defensive halves of the field. They have offensive and defensive roles and are key to the transition game.

Midline: The line that divides the field in half, creating an offensive half and a defensive half. The line extends from sideline to sideline.

Offside: A violation that results from not having three attackers in the offensive end of the field and four defenders in the defensive end of the field. If the offensive team commits the violation, the ball changes possession. If the defending team commits the violation, a 30-second penalty is imposed.

Overhand motion: A variation of the passing or shooting motion. The player passes or shoots with the stick parallel to the body.

Painting the post: A usually very accurate shooting motion where the stick is perpendicular to the ground. The shooting motion is similar to the up-and-down movement of painting a post.

Passing: The technique of throwing the ball to a teammate using the stick in a variety of positions.

Passing lane: Open spaces a cutter can move into to receive a pass.

Penetration: A dodge or movement toward the goal.

Pick: An offensive technique where one player comes to a stationary position, blocking the pathway of a defender.

Player-down defense: The defensive situation that occurs when the offense has gained a player advantage due to a defensive penalty.

Player-to-player defense: A team defensive strategy where every defender is responsible for an opposing offensive player.

Point behind: The area directly behind the goal.

Poke check: A check executed when a player uses his stick head to poke the opposing player. The motion is similar to striking a ball with a pool cue. The top hand is stationary and guides the motion, and the bottom hand drives the stick forward.

Pocket: The portion of the stick head created by the mesh or leather stringing. It's the area the ball settles into for cradling.

Punch and drag: A face-off technique where one player pushes his stick forward to knock his opponent's stick out of the way and then uses his stick to draw the ball backward.

Pushing: A violation that results in a change of possession or technical foul.

Rake: A technique used by the face-off player to sweep the ball out of the face-off toward a teammate or to a strategic area.

Restraining box: The area in the offensive zone that surrounds the crease and extends toward the end lines and sidelines. This is the goal area.

Riding: A special situation where the offense tries to prevent the defense from clearing the ball into the offensive half of the field.

Right behind: The position behind the goal to the goalie's right.

Roll dodge: A dodge in which the first attacker penetrates by spinning past the defender and attacking the goal.

Rotation slide: A defensive slide in which the first defender slides to the ball and rotates away from the ball after a pass has been made.

Scooping: The technique used to gain possession of the ball when it's on the ground.

Screening: An offensive technique in which a player several yards off the crease positions himself between the shooter and the goalie, shielding the vision of the goalie.

Second attacker: The offensive player closest to the first attacker. His role is to provide support by creating dodging space, cutting to the goal, or becoming available for a pass.

Second defender: The defensive player who's in the help position, supporting the first defender and ready to slide if needed.

Set plays: Predetermined plays that use a precribed pattern of movement by players.

Settled clearing: A clear after stoppages of play that begins on the referee's whistle. See also *unsettled clearing*.

Shaft: The part of the stick that a player holds for passing, catching, scooping, and shooting. At one end of the shaft is the head of the stick attached by a screw, and at the other end is a plastic cap that covers the end of the stick.

Shooting: The motion executed by a player where he uses the stick to throw the ball toward the goal in an attempt to score a goal.

Shuffle: A side-to-side movement, which allows the defender to maintain his angle and balance.

Sidearm motion: A variation of the passing or shooting technique where the player moves the stick into a position that's more parallel to the ground than to the player's body.

Sidelines: The lines marking the out-of-bounds area running the length of the field from end line to end line.

Side sprint: Similar to a *shuffle*, but done faster.

Slap check: A stick check used in an attempt to dislodge the ball from the offensive player's stick. The defender uses a quick wrist snap, moving the stick toward the offensive player who's attempting to strike the stick.

Slashing: A personal foul occurring when a player swings his stick and hits another player.

Slide: A technique used by the second and third defenders to support the first defender. When a dodge has been successful, the second defender moves to stop penetration, and the third defender moves to a help position.

Split dodge: A dodge where the offensive player moves laterally in one direction and then quickly changes direction to move laterally in the other direction, switching the stick as the direction changes.

Stack slide: A defensive technique involving two defenders. The first defender takes the ball, and the second defender covers the middle. The rotation switches on a pass. The second defender always covers the middle.

Stick check: A legal defensive technique in which a player uses his stick to hit his opponent's stick in order to dislodge the ball or to prevent his opponent from throwing, shooting, or catching.

Stick on stick: A technique used by the first defender, who keeps his stick on the hands and stick of the first attacker. It's also utilized by all defenders on a "check" call by the goalie.

Substitution box: The area on the sidelines at midfield from which players must make substitions.

Ten-player ride: A defensive strategy in which all offensive players are marked to try to force a turnover.

Third attacker: All offensive players other than the first or second attacker. The job of these players is to create passing lanes, cut to the goal, and maintain field balance.

Third defender: All defensive players other than the first or second defender. The job of these players is to deny the passing lanes, provide communication to players defending the ball, and be ready to execute a second slide to the help position if needed.

Top center: The position outside the restraining lines directly in front of the goalie.

Top left or right: Areas above or just inside the restraining lines to the goalie's left or right.

Transition: The switch from defense to offense and the movement of the ball from the defensive zone to the offensive zone.

Trap: Forcing a player into a closed space, a space where there are multiple defenders, or where offensive options are limited by field boundaries.

Triangle slide: A rotation slide that is part of a six-on-six defense. Players rotate (slide) to help as needed and replace each other.

Tuck: The motion of bringing to ball to the box area and pulling the stick into the body to help shield the ball and the stick from a check.

Underhand motion: A variation of the passing or shooting technique where the player moves the stick more parallel with the body but keeps the stick head below the waist. This motion creates increased power but decreased accuracy for most players.

Unsettled clearing: A clear that occurs when there's a steal, a loose ground ball, or a save. See also *settled clearing*.

V-cut: A movement in which the attacker moves into a defender or a defender's space and then explodes away into open space while moving toward the ball. The path of this motion looks like a V.

Warding off: An illegal motion that occurs when the first attacker uses a one-arm cradle and then uses his free arm to push away the defender's stick.

Weak side: The side of the field opposite the ball.

Wing areas: Areas toward the sidelines along the midfield used during a face-off to line up the wing midfielders.

Wrap check: A stick check used to dislodge the ball. The defender overplays to the stick side of the first attacker and reaches around the midsection of the first attacker with the head and shaft of the stick, making contact with the stick of the first attacker.

Zone defense: A tactic used by a team where the defense is responsible for areas of the defensive half of the field inside the restraining area, instead of marking individual players.

Zone offense: A tactic used by a team where the offense works to overload specific areas in the offensive half of the field.

Resources

Associations and Organizations

American Sport Education Program (ASEP)
1607 N. Market St.
Champaign IL 61820
800-747-5698
Fax: 217-351-2674
E-mail: asep@hkusa.com
www.asep.com
ASEP offers educational courses and resources for coaches, directors, and parents to make sports safer, more enjoyable, and valuable for children and young adults. It also publishes books on coaching youth sports.

National Alliance for Youth Sports (NAYS)
2050 Vista Pkwy.
West Palm Beach FL 33411
800-729-2057; 800-688-KIDS
    (800-688-5437); 561-684-1141
Fax: 561-684-2546
E-mail: nays@nays.org
www.nays.org
NAYS sponsors nine national programs that educate volunteer coaches, parents, youth sport program administrators, and officials about their roles and responsibilities. Their Web site provides information on these education programs, including: PAYS (Parents Association for Youth Sports); NYSCA (National Youth Sports Coaches Association); NYSOA (National Youth Sports Officials Association); START SMART; and the Academy for Youth Sports Administrators.

National Federation of State High School Associations (NFHS)
P.O. Box 690
Indianapolis IN 46206
800-776-3462 (to order rule books);
    317-972-6900
Fax: 317-822-5700
www.nfhs.org
Publishes rule books for high school sports, case books (which supplement rule books), and officials' manuals.

National Lacrosse League (NLL)
1212 Avenue of the Americas,
    5th Fl.
New York NY 10036
917-510-9200
Fax: 917-510-9890
www.nationallacrosse.com
The official site of the National Lacrosse League.

National Youth Sports Safety Foundation (NYSSF)
333 Longwood Ave., Suite 202
Boston MA 02115
617-277-1171
Fax: 617-277-2278
E-mail: NYSSF@aol.com
www.nyssf.org
NYSSF is a nonprofit educational organization whose goal is to reduce the risks of sports injury to young people.

North American Youth Sport Institute (NAYSI)
4985 Oak Garden Dr.
Kernersville NC 27284-9520
800-767-4916; 336-784-4923
Fax: 336-784-5546

www.naysi.com
NAYSI's Web site features information and resources to help teachers, coaches, and other youth leaders, including parents, interact more effectively with children around sports. It includes a resource section that lists books on sports and coaching, as well as two interactive sections where browsers can submit questions on fitness, recreation, and sports. The Web site's newsletter, Sport Scene, focuses on youth programs.

Positive Coaching Alliance (PCA)
c/o Stanford Athletic Dept.
Stanford CA 94305-6150
650-725-0024
Fax: 650-725-7242
E-mail: pca@positivecoach.org
www.positivecoach.org
PCA is transforming youth sports so sports can transform youth.

US Lacrosse
113 W. University Pkwy.
Baltimore MD 21210
410-235-6882
Fax: 410-366-6735
E-mail: info@lacrosse.org
www.lacrosse.org
US Lacrosse is the national governing body of men's and women's lacrosse. It combines the contributions and talents of individuals formerly involved with a number of independent national constituencies, such as the Lacrosse Foundation, the United States Women's Lacrosse Association, the National Junior Lacrosse Association, the United States Lacrosse Officials Association, United States Lacrosse Coaches Association, United States Club Lacrosse Association, the Central Atlantic Lacrosse League, and the National Intercollegiate Lacrosse Officials Association.

Youth Lacrosse USA (YLUSA)
P.O. Box 10588
Greensboro NC 27404-0588
336-215-4955
Fax: 336-854-1065
E-mail: info@youthlacrosseusa.com
www.youthlacrosseusa.com
YLUSA's goals include energizing youth to get involved with and learn to play lacrosse, providing free mini Web sites for YLSUA-registered teams, facilitating communication among coaches and program directors for scheduling, assisting interested parents in developing youth lacrosse programs, providing lacrosse tournament, camp and all-star team opportunities for youth players, and developing an on-line community for youth lacrosse players and program leaders.

Web Sites

Coaching Youth Sports
www.tandl.vt.edu/rstratto/CYS
Virginia Tech's Health and Physical Education program sponsors this Web site, which provides coaches, athletes, and parents with general, rather than sport-specific, information about skills for youth. The site also allows browsers to submit questions.

National Youth Sports Coaches Association (NYSCA)

800-729-2057; 800-688-KIDS
(800-688-5437); 561-684-1141
www.nays.org/coaches/index.cfm
NYSCA trains volunteer coaches in all aspects of working with children and athletics. In addition to training, coaches receive continuing education and insurance coverage and subscribe to a coaching code of ethics.

National Youth Sports Officials Association (NYSOA)

800-729-2057; 800-688-KIDS
(800-688-5437); 561-684-1141
www.nays.org/officials/nysoa.cfm
NYSOA trains volunteer youth sports officials, providing them with information on the skills required, fundamentals of coaching, as well as common problems they may encounter.

Officiating.com

E-mail: Feedback@Officiating.com
www.officiating.com
This Web site offers news, including updates on rule changes, coaching philosophy and mechanics, and discussion boards.

Parents Association for Youth Sports (PAYS)

800-729-2057; 800-688-KIDS
(800-688-5437); 561-684-1141
www.nays.org/pays/index.cfm
PAYS provides material and information for youth sports programs to help teach parents about their roles and responsibilities in children's sports activities.

United States Club Lacrosse Association (USCLA)

www.uscla.com
The United States Club Lacrosse Association is the oldest and most prestigious Club Lacrosse League in the world. Teams presently range from Boston, Massachusetts, through central New York and the mid-Atlantic states to southern Maryland. There are plans in the near future to expand into the Midwest and South with the hope of developing a true national club league. Toward this end, the USCLA has supported the concept of the establishment of a National Governing Body.

US Lacrosse Youth Council

www.lacrosse.org/yth_council.html
The US Lacrosse Youth Council is charged with promoting girls' and boys' lacrosse in a safe and sportsmanlike environment. The Youth Council has established a Code of Conduct that emphasizes sportsmanship to players, coaches, parents, spectators, and officials. Attendees and participants in US Lacrosse Youth Council events are required to sign a contract and pledge to "Honor the Game."

Lacrosse Stores and Publications

Bacharach

802 Gleneagles Ct.
Towson MD 21286
800-726-2468
Fax: 410-321-0720
E-mail: bachrasin@aol.com
www.bacharach.com
Lacrosse store and catalog company.

E-Lacrosse
www.e-lacrosse.com
The on-line lacrosse supersite and store. They have an on-line store with books.

Great Atlantic Lacrosse Company
Old Wyler's Dock
Box 16872
Chapel Hill NC 27516
800-955-3876
Fax: 800-204-1198
www.lacrosse.com
They produce a catalog and sponsor many events.

Inside Lacrosse
P.O. Box 5570
Towson MD 21285
410-583-8180
Fax: 410-296-8296
www.insidelacrosse.com
A lacrosse magazine and on-line site.

Lacrosse Magazine
US Lacrosse
113 W. University Pkwy.
Baltimore MD 21210
410-235-6882
Fax: 410-366-6735
E-mail: info@lacrosse.org
www.lacrosse.org/magazine.html
Published eight times a year. Members receive a subscription to *Lacrosse Magazine*.

Lacrosse Unlimited
2292 Hempstead Turnpike
East Meadow NY 11554
877-932-5229; 800-366-5299
www.lacrosseunltd.com
Lacrosse store, on-line and catalog.

Lax World Lacrosse Superstore
800-PLAY-LAX (800-752-9529)
Fax: 410-561-7278
E-mail: ptmailorder@laxworld.com
www.playlax.com
Lacrosse store, retail and on-line.

360Lacrosse.com
www.360lacrosse.com
On-line store and news center.

Index

Numbers in **bold** refer to pages with illustrations. The glossary and resources have not been indexed.

Acknowledgments

Thanks to my coaches over the years—especially John Grubb—whose knowledge and love of the game helped me learn and love it too. Thanks to all my teammates—you've given me many special memories. Finally, thanks to the youth players and coaches—you've given us the chance to share our love of the game.

Greg Murrell

Thanks to my wife Debra for her support and her countless hours of typing during the writing of this book. Thanks also to all of the parents, coaches, and players who have given us the opportunity to continue to learn and to be a small part of their lives.

Jim Garland

About the Authors

Greg Murrell played college lacrosse at Salisbury University. He is a lacrosse coach with the North Harford Hawks of Maryland, who were state finalists in 1994, state champions in 1995, and county champions in 1994, 1995, 1998, 1999, and 2000. He has been a member of the Harford County Lacrosse Camp staff for eleven years, and is the current director of Motion Concepts Sports Camps, which offer coach and player clinics. He also teaches middle school science and is completing his master's degree in administration at Loyola College.

Jim Garland graduated from Towson University and is a member of its Athletic Hall of Fame. He holds bachelor's and master's degrees in physical education and a doctoral degree in child and youth studies. He has been an elementary physical education teacher for over thirty years, coached youth and high school sports, and served as a clinician on the local, state, and national level. He founded the Motion Masters and Motion Concepts Sports Camps. He is the author of *Great Baseball Drills: The Baffled Parent's Guide* and *Great Basketball Drills: The Baffled Parent's Guide*.